After Summerhill

What Happened to the Children of Britain's Most Radical School?

by
Hussein Lucas

Dedicated to the memory of Elizabeth Pascall

First published in 2011

Copyright © Hussein Lucas 2011

ISBN: 978-1-84289-052-3

Printed and bound in the UK

Herbert Adler
Publishing
www.herbertadler.co.uk

Acknowledgements

I would like to express my special thanks to the following individuals and organisations:

Albert Lamb for his help, encouragement, introductions and editorial input into several of the interviews, which first appeared in Friends of Summerhill Trust [FOST] magazine.

Hylda Sims for her helpful suggestions and introductions to other Summerhillians.

Freer Spreckley and the Friends of Summerhill Trust for encouragement and support.

Zoë Readhead for her time and help.

To the many former teachers, parents, houseparents and pupils who gave up their time to be interviewed but whose interviews, for reasons of space, do not appear in this book.

To those individuals whose interviews appear on the following pages, since without their time and input there would not be a book.

To Jonathan Croall whose biography of Neill provided me with much useful background information.

I also wish to acknowledge Jeremy Mulford for his invaluable editorial input and helpful suggestions, and my publisher for his constant support, enthusiasm, advice and encouragement and most of all for his belief that this was a book that should be published.

About the Author

Hussein Lucas has a longstanding interest in education and was for many years involved with a number of progressive schools and therapeutic communities. He has maintained a special interest in Summerhill.

He has written short stories, poems and plays for newspapers, magazines, radio and theatre festivals and contributed to alternative education magazines including the *Friends of Summerhill Trust Journal.*

Contents

Introduction

Like Plato's *Republic,* Thomas More's *Utopia,* William Morris's *Nowhere* and Aldous Huxley's *Island,* Summerhill is a small place but a big idea, the principal difference being that Summerhill really exists and has done so for the best part of a century. In 2011, the year of this book's publication, the school will be celebrating its 90th anniversary.

So much has been written about Summerhill School that one inevitably asks why such a small place has evoked so much controversy. Curiously, it still has the power to provoke strong reactions, even in an age when many of the things it originally stood against are no longer in place. In the past 20 to 30 years there have been many important changes in the state education system that would seem to indicate a move towards increasing liberalism. These include the abolition of corporal punishment and a growing sense of the rights of children in general.

One of the questions that inevitably arise when assessing Summerhill, is whether these developments have made Summerhill redundant, in that the rest of the educational world would seem to have caught up with it. Not so. It is an indication of the depth of the radicalism in Summerhill's approach that in 1999, the Department for Education and Employment served a Notice of Complaint against the school after an inspection, effectively undermining its philosophy and practice and demanding change. The outcome was a court hearing where the school was able, despite such formidable opposition, to vindicate its principles and the Notice of Complaint was withdrawn.

In considering these changes one needs to look beneath the surface. Whilst ostensibly there have been improvements in the circumstances of those being educated, there is still a powerful emphasis on success, largely of a material kind, and achievement, of a formal academic nature, that many sense is being imposed at the expense of individual and social development, or in other words, the development of a rounded human personality. In fact, there is evidence of a growing awareness amongst university graduates that the received wisdom – the harder you study and the more qualifications you pile up, the more likely you will be to obtain fulfilling and financially rewarding work – is a myth. And, far from having developed an enhanced capacity for the enjoyment of life (which is one measure of happiness and indeed intelligence), many feel demotivated, frustrated and, in fact, cheated.

Whilst not wishing to deny the importance of formal learning, my experience of Summerhill, which is based around meeting and getting to know quite a few of its former pupils, has led me to the view that this school has succeeded and survived, in no small degree, by virtue of its ability to *encourage* (in the sense of giving courage) and enable its pupils to engage with the world in a positive, creative and regenerative way that is, in the main, characterised by a highly developed nose for the authentic in all things, and a mature social consciousness.

If I were to be asked, what is the key, salient feature that sums up the distinctive nature of the Summerhill experience over the past nine decades, it is the virtual absence of fear: fear of failure; fear of authority; fear of social ostracism; fear of life and the consequent failure to engage with it with a feeling of optimism and a positive outlook.

Economic and political insecurity, combined with an increasingly unrealistic longing to create a risk-free environment in which someone else is always to blame or be held accountable, are characteristics of modern life. With an unpressured childhood behind them, Summerhillians, it seems to me, are far better equipped than most to deal confidently with what the *real* world has to throw at them.

Hussein Lucas

Publisher's Preface

When Hussein Lucas first told me that he was writing a book about the lives of former pupils at Summerhill, I was interested – for a number of reasons. Firstly, some years ago we had both become involved in an alternative school, which, although it had been a largely positive experience for us both, we felt had left certain things to be desired. Also, having recently left my job as a university educator, where I had come to question many of the underlying precepts of our normative educational culture and started a new career as a publisher, this seemed an appropriate sort of project to become involved in.

My own experiences of primary and secondary education had not been what I would want to repeat, or subject anyone else to, and accordingly I had developed a long-standing interest in alternatives to mainstream education. I knew that the school had a philosophy, going back to its origins in the 1920s, of never requiring a child to attend lessons, and this idea struck me as astoundingly radical. I felt that if this idea had prevailed at my grammar school I would never have learned a thing, yet I was forgetting that the context was one that was very different from Summerhill. And so I read Hussein's original manuscript with some anticipation, not without an element of vicarious curiosity as to what the products of this most untypical school would be like: uneducated, wild, anarchic, innocents abroad in the world...?

What struck me, as I read about their lives and attitudes, was how sane they all seemed, marked by such qualities as a sense of balance, consideration for others and, above all, honesty. This was endorsed by the experience of speaking with a number of them subsequently. They come across as people who seem to understand that others have a point of view that is important whether you agree with them or not. They might be liberal or socialist in their outlook, but there is no trace of bigotry.

Something else that struck me was that they are people who are not scared of the world. They might find it strange or even

13

incomprehensible at times, but they seem to feel free to encounter it and make something of it without the encumbrance of fear, whether it be of failure or of the world itself. Furthermore, I would surmise that in most cases, this lack of fear has helped them, without exception, make a success of their lives and prevail.

Looking back on my own education, where the utter suppression of rights, physical assault in the form of corporal punishment and Darwinian survival mechanisms were the accepted order of the day, I now see that an education that is rooted in coercion and the rule of fear is immensely harmful, even if people manage to overcome it, as the indomitable human spirit has a way of doing.

At the heart of the Summerhill formula is respect for the child, which was and is a visionary approach. The school is an environment where one is answerable to one's peers through the medium of the school parliament. It is a place where the lack of adult coercion gives one the freedom to find out who you are, away from the pressures of family life. It is in effect a social enterprise more than an education in the formal sense. I'm not surprised that so many Summerhill kids could not wait to get back to school after the holidays.

In effect, Summerhill is founded on creating the opportunity for the individual to develop organically as a person within the framework of the belief that people are fundamentally good, and that, allowed to develop in a free environment, they will eventually find their way. This was Neill's greatest accomplishment – to trust children in the belief that they are fundamentally good; an idea that still fills many people with dread and apprehension to this day.

I would say that Summerhill's influence has not been nearly as pervasive as it could or should have been. I feel sure that such an environment placed away, as it is, from the often negative influence of dysfunctional families or a violent or morally corrupting social environment, could go a long way to helping rescue the growing legions of delinquent or feral kids, from a life that might well end in disaster.

In an age where education seems to have lost so much of its idealism and been reduced to another manifestation of consumerism through such impositions as the national curriculum and government league tables, Summerhill is a beacon of hope. Surely, in moments of lucidity, most people would agree that the ultimate criterion of an education is its ability to release the potential of the individual to lead his or her life to the best of their human potential. In this equation, happiness, sound motivation and a sense of wellbeing must be at the top of the list. Read on.

John Adler

After
Summerhill

Summerhill and A.S. Neill

Alexander Sutherland Neill was born in Kingsmuir, Scotland, in 1883, the third of eight surviving children of the village schoolmaster, or dominie. After a rather unhappy and academically inauspicious childhood, he left school at 14 to work firstly as a clerk, then as a draper's assistant. Neither of these jobs proving a success, he was taken on by his father as a pupil-teacher – that is, one giving lessons to younger children in return for further education for himself. Neill continued in this mode until 1908 when, at the age of 25, he gained a place at Edinburgh University. He graduated with an MA in English. A burgeoning career in publishing and journalism was cut short in 1914 by the outbreak of war.

Having failed his army medical, Neill was appointed acting head of Gretna Village School. Here he started to put into practice and develop his innovative ideas on education. Out of this experience came the first of his twenty books, *A Dominie's Log* (published 1916), which became an immediate best-seller and made him well-known.

A subsequent army medical examination passed Neill as fit for general military service and he was called up for training in 1917. Whilst on leave he met and came under the influence of Homer Lane, who ran his Little Commonweath for delinquent boys and girls using a system of self-government. This had a profound effect on shaping Neill's approach to the community aspect of education. Lane also introduced him to the work of Freud and other psychoanalysts. Neill's second book, *A Dominie Dismissed*, was published that year and like its predecessor sold well. It was agreed that Neill would join the staff of Lane's community as soon as the war had ended, but before he could do so the Little Commonwealth was closed down.

Neill's third book, *The Booming of Bunkie*, was published in 1919. In that same year – the opportunity of working directly with Lane having been denied him (though the relationship continued) – Neill joined the staff of King Alfred School, Hampstead, at that time the most progressive school in England. It was not progressive enough – or perhaps radical enough – for Neill, however, and he left after five terms following a disagreement over self-government.

One of the children in his class at King Alfred was Walter Neustatter whose mother, Lilian, an Australian of Irish descent married to a German eye surgeon, had been visiting her sister in England when war broke out and decided to stay on. She was impressed by this unusual man and his ideas about education, and on her return to Germany invited him to stay with her and her husband, Otto.

In 1921, whilst staying with the Neustatters in Hellerau, a suburb of Dresden, Neill visited the nearby Dalcroze School, which had been founded before the war by Émile Jaques-Dalcroze as a centre for the teaching of Eurythmics. Christine Baer, an American and former pupil of Dalcroze, who now ran the centre, was also taken with Neill's educational ideas and suggested he should start an international school in an unused wing of the building. A limited liability company was formed and Neill invested what savings he had in what was to be the first "Summerhill". That year also saw the publication of his fourth and fifth books, *A Dominie in Doubt* and *Carroty Broon*. Neill was thus already comparatively famous as a writer and thinker by the time he started his great adventure in education.

Elizabeth Pascall
1921-23

Elizabeth Pascall attended the International School (considered to be the first Summerhill) at the beginning of its development, when Neill did not have a clear idea of what he wanted to achieve, apart from "freedom from compulsion" and self-government. Elizabeth was thus very much a guinea pig, in that not only was she the first female pupil, but the total complement after she had arrived was a mere three pupils. It was a time of experimentation – albeit derived from Neill's experiences at Gretna, The Little Commonwealth and King Alfred – of organic development rather than intricate planning, when the seeds of what Neill later felt able to call a "demonstration" school were being sown. But at that time there was no way of knowing whether the school would even survive.

Known at that time as Betty Mortimer, Elizabeth was born in Ilford in 1908 and brought up in Harrogate. Her father was a chemist by profession and a well-known lay preacher who also served on the town council and was a founder member of the Rotary Club. Her mother was a Swedenborgian [a follower of the Swedish mystic, Swedenborg] who came from a long line of artists. Although not wealthy the family managed to live well. "It was a culturally rich background with masses of books in the house. Sometimes my parents would forego lunch in order to buy a book."

Elizabeth was an only child but very happy. "I was always treated as an equal by my parents. They would discuss everything with me – art and life. I was never pushed out. Because I was an only child I spent a lot of time with adults. My parents had a lot of very interesting acquaintances such as Keir Hardie, Ruskin, and Margaret McMillan who, with her sister Rachel, founded the nursery school movement in the United Kingdom."

At the age of ten, Betty, as she was then known, went away to a Quaker boarding school near Middlesborough. Before that she had been to various local day schools. "A school down the road had refused to take me because I was a tradesman's daughter. Then, when my father became chairman of the local education committee, they changed their mind, but he wasn't going to accept after that rebuff. Not that he minded so much. There was no bitterness about it. He was an amusing man, full of fun."

Betty was at the Quaker boarding school from 1919 to 1921. She remembers enjoying the Friends meetings, which she still attends, but not much else. "It was a coeducational school and I disliked the smell and roughness of the Yorkshire boys. I felt ill-at-ease with boys *en masse*. It was very stark after home, but I learnt then that for children physical surroundings are not all-important. What they need most is human love. I was very homesick there.

"Mother knew that I was becoming increasingly unhappy at the Quaker school. Then one day, one of the boys, who was slightly mental, exposed himself to me. This was not a real shock because I had often seen my father naked, but I complained, probably more for the sensation of something happening. I was making the best of the incident. My parents guessed this but were quite prepared for me to use it as an excuse for leaving the school. So I went home."

Betty's mother had by then read Neill's first two books, *A Dominie's Log* and *A Dominie Dismissed*, and been impressed. "I had read *A Dominie's Log* myself and liked it. Dr Boyd, a friend who lived in Harrogate, told Mother that Neill was coming to stay with him to make arrangements for taking his elder son, Derrick, to Hellerau. So my parents invited the Boyds and Neill to lunch in a private room in a café in the town. I sat next to Neill and immediately liked him very much. He was very easy to get on with. He asked me what I wanted to be and I told him I wanted to be a missionary, probably to impress. He made some comment, I don't remember what exactly, that made me think perhaps he hadn't been so impressed."

Elizabeth's parents decided to send her to Germany. "At that time it was almost unheard of for any but the wealthy even to visit abroad, so it took a lot of trust for my parents to send me. But Neill inspired that sort of trust.

"Hellerau was a beautiful model village. There was a purpose-built hostel to stay in with single bedrooms which I much appreciated after the dormitory at the Quaker school. The natural surroundings were wonderful, and the evenings in the pine forests had a mystical quality.

"For me, personally, the importance was the whole ambience, the whole thing – the school, the music, the beauty, and being able to develop in a place in which I was really happy. On the whole each day was a nice day, and it was the first time it had happened to me in school life. And also not being afraid of what the next moment would hold, which is more than you can say about most schools."

Neill was much loved. "Everybody liked him, children and adults. He treated everyone the same, regardless of age." But though very loving with children he rejected physical contact. "I think he was afraid it would be misunderstood." The one thing Betty found disrespectful was being referred to as a kid. "I've never liked that term."

By then Neill's books were well-known and there were a lot of visitors to Hellerau among whom were the poet Edwin Muir and his wife, Willa, who taught Betty English. "Willa Muir was a very nice woman and a good writer herself of course. I had lessons one-to-one mostly." Sometimes girls of other nationalities would attend in order to learn English. "That of course was one of the great joys of being at Hellerau – mixing with different nationalities. I had one very good friend who was later killed in a concentration camp because she was Jewish. She was Hungarian. A lovely girl. Neill broke the news of her death to me. He was very fond of her."

The lessons with Willa took the form of reading and discussions. "I don't think we wrote any essays. I've still got a couple of letters I wrote at the time and they were extraordinarily illiterate. I'm horrified that I wrote so badly. Yet Neill's contention was that you'd do it when you wanted to, and this was borne out. The stories I wrote when I was 16, only a couple of years later, were perfectly literate.

"Whatever you wanted to learn, Neill would try to provide someone to teach you, though the teachers at Hellerau weren't chosen by Neill, they just turned up. There were a number of political refugees in Germany at that time, from places like Hungary. My Latin teacher was Hungarian, so I learned to speak it with a Hungarian accent."

No one adult, Elizabeth felt, was a particularly big influence, though Frau Doctor [later to be known to generations of Summerhillians as Mrs Lins – a contraction of Lilian Neustatter], who became matron of the hostel, was important. "I enjoyed helping her. She was companionable."

As for Neill he was always writing or making things and he did private psychology classes for the girls at the dancing school. "Other children began to come and we had regular school meetings – *Schulgemeinde*. Nothing was compulsory and we made up our own rules, very much like it is today. Neill wanted children to have a feeling of self-discipline; to be aware of the consequences of their actions."

Elizabeth remembers Neill as a very good instinctive psychologist. "During one of my visits to the school, after it had moved to Lyme Regis, I attended a general meeting. A child had done something, I don't remember what, and the whole school was very down on him. Then Neill got up and confessed to a misdemeanour of his own. At the time I felt rather irritated with him. I didn't see the point of his interruption until it dawned on me later that what he'd done was to direct the attention of the whole meeting away from the child and towards himself. It worked. Everybody forgot the original culprit and turned on Neill. The look of relief on that child's face was marvellous. This was typical of Neill. He had seen that this child's suffering was unbearable and acted in the most inspired way to relieve it."

However, Elizabeth felt that Neill had never got over his Calvinist upbringing and went on fighting his own battles, often against a mythical *them*. "He tended to presume in advance that certain people would be very critical of what he was doing, often quite without reason. But he was unique, a spearhead for many innovations. Though he was never given to organisation, he did have a great impact on people.

"But, in order to get his point across he would use exaggeration and some people were worried by this. The danger with that type of approach is that it can seem as if you're only trying to shock. And he did. He shocked them into thinking. Some found him merely outrageous, but a lot of others found he opened their minds and that was helpful.

"Having watched his impact on the outside world I found that the great importance was his breaking down of the barrier of thought. He managed to make people take a different attitude. You might almost call it lateral thinking in modern jargon. In a way the fact that he got stuck with the one idea was perhaps necessary for that one idea to be developed."

Elizabeth met Neill's parents when they visited Hellerau. "Neill has written about the difficult time he had with his father in his youth; he was a very small, neat man and you could tell that perhaps he had the capacity to be quite stern, but I found both the parents delightful. Perhaps they had mellowed with age. They seemed very proud of their son."

There were no compulsory lessons. "Nobody taught you anything unless you wanted it. It wasn't strange not being made to go to lessons or to do homework: it seemed reasonable. It was a relief. But I was very grateful when I grew older for what I'd got from the Quaker school. I had all my basic education there. I could read and do sums in my head and long division, that sort of thing. And then of course I followed it up in later years with reading and writing.

"The boys worked with Neill making things. He gave me a few maths lessons. I could have as much privacy as I wanted. I could go to my room and read and nobody bothered me. Sometimes I'd sit in Neill's room, watching him type. He would read out extracts from *A Dominie Abroad*, in which I appear under the pseudonym of Mary, which I chose myself, and ask me if I liked it."

It is Elizabeth's belief that teaching did not actually interest Neill. "He didn't really believe in teaching you anything. He believed you should be left to find out. I think he would be very happy to tell you how to use an encyclopedia or a dictionary, but he felt that if you were told something, an historical fact, it really wasn't necessarily going to help you much. If you wanted to know and you looked it up, then that would help you."

All the adults were called by their surnames in those days, with the prefix Mr or Mrs or their German equivalents, but Neill was always plain Neill. "I didn't compare him to my previous teachers. He just was Neill. He was never the headmaster. If someone asked you for the headmaster, you had to think before you realised, Oh, he means Neill. He was just Neill, and a great friend of course."

There was dancing in the hostel nearly every evening to a wind-up gramophone. "Foxtrots were all the rage and we had a good collection of records. Neill loved dancing but he was an appalling dancer; he had trouble with his feet. Most days I went to Eurythmics and dance practice. I loved it, although I was aware I didn't have the physique to become a professional dancer."

The New Psychology was a hot point of discussion at that time. "There was a strong feeling of renewal and rebirth. No more war, the modern psychology would solve everything. It was going to transform the world. Everything was going to be so wonderful, but it was felt it would be awful if it ever got into the hands of the medical profession, which of course it has."

All the people who stayed at or visited Hellerau seemed to have something special. "I particularly remember the Muirs and going to a fascinating talk given by a visiting theosophist. I spent a lot of time talking to adults, as I had done at home. We went to concerts in Dresden. The dancing school itself put on an early production of one of Bartok's ballets, which really awakened me to music."

Inflation started to worsen while Elizabeth was there. "I remember we would get twice as many German notes for the same amount of English money in the afternoon as in the morning. I had to take a large handbag to the bank with me to put all the notes in. If you had English currency to exchange you were really well off. I bought a sewing machine, a gold watch and a really swish velvet hat – all out of my one pound a month pocket-money."

There was none of the sexual promiscuity that opponents of coeducational boarding schools warned against. "We were all very careful in those days, to a degree which people today would find difficult to understand. When I was 13, I acquired a German boyfriend, Ulrich. He was very handsome. Neill took me aside one day and warned me about the risk of becoming pregnant. I was shocked. We had not the remotest idea of having sex."

There was a folk school, the Neue Schule, in the same building as the International School, attended by local German children. "It was very liberal by German standards, but strict by ours. They mixed with us socially and were fascinated by us, for apparently we could do what we wanted. It was a marvellous time. I felt for once I was able to be myself, but that was largely because of the dancing. I had girlfriends from the dance and folk schools. I read enormously. Neill had all O'Henry's books: he considered him the world's greatest short-story writer."

As well as literature, music and dance, there was plenty of other artistic activity. "We painted the walls with murals. There was so much going on. The time, the place, the people made it as good as a university."

Elizabeth left when the school moved to Austria. It was partly the distance from home, resulting in increased fees, coinciding with her father changing his profession. He had begun studying for the bar, which meant a reduced income. "I had loved the atmosphere and being allowed to develop without let or hindrance. I left school with great confidence. I never was a teenager in the sense that I had no self-consciousness. I never thought, What do other people think about me? I was quite capable of looking after myself and taking responsibility for younger children. On my last summer holiday – I was 14 – I returned to England in charge of a ten-year-old girl. The journey took about 36 hours in those days. We'd been put in the wrong coach at Dresden and consequently missed our boat. I didn't have any feeling of panic. The station master pointed us out to two Englishmen who'd also been stranded, one of whom knew the other girl's father. They lent us the money to stay at a hotel and took us out to the cinema in the evening. I had the confidence to trust these men, but I told my companion to stick close to me and then all would be well, which it was. That confidence came partly from my father – 'At least you tried,' he would say when I made a mistake

– but it was also increased by going to Neill's school and living away from home in a foreign country."

The one thing Elizabeth feels she may have missed out on by undergoing this type of education is concentration. "All my life I have never been able to stick at things for long. I feel I've never done anything really thoroughly, but this may have come from natural disposition rather than any deficiency in my education. The important thing about teaching is not to tell you things, but to have your natural abilities brought out. Neill gave me the ability to learn by living: not to be afraid of life."

After Summerhill

After returning from Germany I did a year of private tuition for my matriculation. It was very concentrated work and I found it rather a strain. I fainted during one of my exams, which rather threw all the others out of the window. I never found out how well I'd done in those I did take. My mother later met the invigilator who told her there was no point trying to force a child into an academic mould when they weren't given to it, and mother suggested I might do drama.

I enrolled for the drama course at the London Poly. I had problems with the other girls. They found me peculiar and I thought the things that interested them rather a bore. I always found going on about boys silly. Extraordinarily silly. They had all been to girls-only schools. I thought them immature, but they thought me unsophisticated. And they were right. There were an awful lot of things I didn't know because of having been out of the country.

We had one Chinese man who came to our speech-training classes and I befriended him and through him got to know a lot of other international students at the Friendship Club. I met Krishna Menon there.

London was very entertaining in the twenties. I went to see the first talkie, *The Singing Fool* – which predated *The Jazz Singer* – and

Fred and Adèle Astaire on stage in *Lady Be Good*. The training I got at drama school was very useful because I taught speech to foreigners in years afterwards. The public speaking lessons were also useful. I learned how to arrange my notes and make a speech in five minutes complete with beginning, middle and end. Another student at the same time was Margery Allingham, the mystery writer, who designed and made sets for us. I had only been there a year when the principal got taken ill. The course was disbanded and she died shortly after. I was offered the chance of going to France.

After a short stay in France I went to Switzerland to teach in a convalescent home for children recovering from TB. I gave individual tuition but got the sack for not teaching children who didn't want to be taught. However, not everyone disapproved of this attitude. At least one parent was grateful and said so. Obviously Neill influenced me in my approach. I had great success with one pupil who was terribly lacking in self-confidence and living in the shadow of her elder sister. She felt she could do nothing right, then one day I added up a sum wrongly and she, very tentatively, corrected me. I wasn't at all embarrassed by this, as many teachers would have been, but instead admitted my mistake and congratulated her. From that moment on her confidence grew in leaps and bounds. It's important for everyone to demonstrate they can be wrong and that it doesn't matter. Children gain confidence from this. It's also important to be patient. I never saw either my father or Neill lose their temper.

I returned to London where I worked initially as a private secretary and then as a publicity agent for a film company. Both these jobs were very interesting, but when Lloyd George started canvassing for young people to help organise new Young Liberal Party associations I applied for a job and got it. This is where my public speaking lessons proved invaluable. At 19 I was the youngest political organiser in the country. My area was the South West. I travelled by train throughout Devon and Cornwall, Gloucester, Dorset, Hampshire and Wiltshire, generally staying in a town for a week helping to organise a Young Liberal 'do' and persuading people to come to it and join up. I'd speak and organise other guest speakers. In this way I was sometimes able to suggest my own father. His fee was paid by Central Office. The job came to an end when Lloyd George, who was putting a lot of his own money into the venture, decided he could no longer support it. I spoke for my father, who was the Liberal candidate for Bournemouth, in the 1929 general election. This was the so-called 'Flappers Election': the first time women of 21 were allowed to vote.

I was invited to Holland to speak to Young Liberals over there. I met a Dutch lawyer and got married. My mother approved because he was so suitable. Nine months later I gave birth to a daughter. My husband was domineering, like many Dutch men of that period, and it took a long time before I found the strength to stand up to him. The marriage lasted 10 years, ending just at the beginning of the Second World War. I had to visit Holland to get my divorce. On the way back we passed through a minefield and three weeks later the German invasion of Holland took place.

I got a job as secretary in a Rotary office, just me and three thousand men, and then moved back into public speaking. I worked for the Ministry of Information and an Anglo-American friendship organisation. I was based in London in a flat in Russell Court. I was paid four pounds a week. Two pounds went in rent so I relied on being taken out to dinner. I was there all through the bombing. Even today if a plane flies low overhead or an ambulance siren goes off, I find it difficult. I trusted almost totally on my intuition to see me through.

I married again in 1947, to Sydney Pascall, and my son was born in 1948. Sydney was much older than I in years but young in spirit. We were very happy together. Two and a half years later he died. In 1955 I married again, for the third time. He turned out to be an alcoholic. It was the first time I'd encountered alcoholism and it was very difficult to cope with.

I decided to send my son to a boarding school, partly to get him away from his stepfather. I think it depends on the child and the circumstances whether it is good to send a child away to school. An only child can get stuck too much into habits which can make him unflexible – and I mean unflexible not inflexible. My son was very happy at his prep school; however, two terms in a public school were disastrous. He developed a stammer, so I took him away and sent him to a Quaker school, which was much more satisfactory. If your attitude to the child as a parent is really loving, you can't go so far wrong. I never shouted at my children, rarely gave them a command and when I did it was so unusual they accepted it. But children do need support. I would not send a child away to school before the age of 11 or 12, and if the home is stable, then 16 is a suitable age to go away to college.

A good school, I believe, is one which gives children opportunity to spread their wings. You never can tell with children when they're going to change. And one of the important things which very few teachers seem to realise is that children change constantly. When my children came home from their boarding schools for the holidays, I never presumed that because they liked sugar in their tea when they went away they liked it when they came back. I always started afresh and found it was a very much easier thing rather than trying to say, 'You always used to...' Always is a word that perhaps ought to be taken out of the vocabulary because you should be prepared for change. Neill understood this. He understood children very well, partly because he never grew up himself, but I think that's true of all good teachers. Good teachers nearly always have a childish side. After all, Christ said it, didn't he?

I've spent a good deal of my life in the company of children and young people. I worked for a time as the warden of a ballet school in London. When I was 60 I moved into my present home in Gloucestershire and began taking in children for short visits – eight or so at a time. They came from Germany, France, Holland; partly to improve their English, partly for a holiday. It was very successful; some of them had simply been under too much pressure and needed to unwind. I gave them the space to do this. In the free atmosphere of the home, they lost much of their tensions. The parents of one boy who had seemed completely bored during his time with me told me many years later that this holiday had been the turning-point in his life. I was astonished. Many of my former students and house guests still write to me regularly and invite me to stay with them. Some still come here on visits.

Neill's school gave me the confidence and ability to go on learning. I still have an enquiring mind. I enjoy practical work as well, acquiring new skills, and I've always enjoyed cooking, sewing and knitting. I was never bored. I can't say I've ever been bored in my life, apart from a few small pockets of boredom. I have always been good at entertaining myself, and sociable as well. I was happy either way. The school definitely helped with my attitude to children. General Meetings were an extremely important component: an excellent way of learning to understand other people's points of view and resolving disputes. Schools should practise democracy in this form. When I visited Lyme Regis and saw Derrick Boyd, who was then in his teens, chairing a meeting, I was impressed by his skill and confidence which had grown so much since I had last seen him as a nine-year-old.

I think Neill was right in his belief that a child will, if left alone, learn perfectly well when it wants to. It's true of all children. Even in ordinary schools, if left to some extent alone, not too much harassed, or made a fool of by the teachers, they will suddenly at 12 or thereabouts start learning. But you don't have to leave them entirely alone if they're normal children. I think leaving children to come and go to lessons is based on children who have been damaged, over-pushed or whatever. But really if a teacher's good, a child should want to go to his lessons. In fact I'm not at all sure that the lecture method isn't the best way for teaching, so that children do their work and then have lectures for stimulation. But I'm not sure. Any method that seems good is valuable. I don't think anything dogmatic is right, and that was where I quarrelled with Neill a bit, because I thought he was dogmatic. Even as a child I felt it very much, although of course I couldn't have put it in words quite like that.

The greatest danger with a school like Neill's is the staff, many of whom have their own problems to resolve. It is important to remember that in a free school the teacher cannot be free, but on the contrary has to be more disciplined than the average teacher.

Postscript

In 2006, Elizabeth moved from her home in Gloucestershire to live with her daughter in London. She continued to write and publish poetry until her death in 2009, at the age of 99.

Brian Anscombe
1925-31

Following the French occupation of the Ruhr in 1923, and the consequent worsening of the economic and political situation in Dresden, Neill moved the International School to Sonntagsberg in Austria. However, in 1924, after mounting local opposition and the collapse of the bank in which he'd lodged his savings, Neill decided to return to England, with Lilian Neustatter and five pupils, and found premises in Lyme Regis in a house built on "Summer Hill".

When Brian Anscombe arrived at Summerhill in 1925 it was beginning to take in more "problem" children, including casualties from the English public school system, as well as those who were sent for more positive reasons. The following piece, beginning with his unaccompanied arrival at Summerhill at the age of ten, was written by Brian Anscombe.

I was told I was going to be met at Axminster, a little junction near Lyme Regis. There were only two people on the platform: one was the porter, the other a rather nondescript-looking fellow in an old raincoat. That was Neill – quite unlike my preconceived notion of a headmaster.

In those days Lyme was a small attractive seaside resort. Summerhill was situated on the comparatively undeveloped east side, enjoying a superb exclusive site some 200 feet above sea level, with a terrific view over the town and the whole of Lyme Bay. The house was a three-storey Georgian-style building with a semi-basement housing Neill's workshop. A small nearly-level circular lawn and drive were in front, and a fine grass tennis court had been cut into the sloping grounds at the rear. There were enough tall trees available for climbing.

One of my earliest memories is of a 13-year-old Mary Artner rushing around swinging a bell and shouting *Schulgemeinde*. Meetings were far less formalised than they are today, and invariably took place in Neill's sitting room. Owing primarily to the small numbers – about 10 kids and three or four staff – I believe that, for a while at least, there was not any regular office of chairman. What usually happened was that the person calling the meeting took on this role. The majority of meetings were called as needed, to deal with complaints or other matters arising. It seemed quite a lot of meetings were called, as there were among us a few who broke out at times, and in doing so sometimes upset the well-being of others. In such cases there were not normally any penalties imposed by vote of the meeting, although an aggressor might occasionally be required to compensate the injured party. Talking over such happenings in the meeting was the usual way. Neill sometimes put his oar in from a psychological standpoint, but freedom and understanding was seen, in time, to perform its gentle magic.

I can't recall any rules, though as time went on a few most probably evolved: bedtimes for example. Neill of course maintained his mandatory ban on going down town in the mornings, from Monday to Friday.

Lessons could be found – some at least. After a few weeks mucking about, and being interested in chemistry, I attached myself to Corky's [George Corkhill] class. He seemed to be available almost every morning and I was frequently the only one present in his class. I learnt a great deal about chemistry from Corky. Later I joined Jonesie's [Bronwen Jones] maths class, but after a while, not being able to fathom the mystique of calculus, dropped out of it.

Friday was pocket-money day. The going rate in 1925 was derived from the formula of half your age minus a penny. Thus at 10 I received fourpence, but it was surprising what could be bought for fourpence especially if one liked sweets. Naturally there had to be a sweet shop not too far away, and there was: the tiniest sweet shop I've ever seen, Barry's, run by a less than affable woman. It was just possible for two to get into it before it became overcrowded.

Saturday night was cinema night, and soon after 7.30 the whole school trooped down the hill to the Picture House at the eastern end of the promenade. I believe the back part jutted out over the sea. These were the silent days, and the menu was predominantly classic westerns featuring well-known idols such as Tom Mix, Hoot Gibson and Jack Hoxy. The silence was filled by the indefatigable efforts of the lady pianist at one side of the screen. Her rather predictable repertoire never failed to match the mood of the film and its changing scenes. The front row seats were I think fourpence for kids, and during the interval there would be a rush for the foyer to buy large ice-cream cornets costing a penny-halfpenny. This was superb stuff, the real thing, not ersatz. The same could be obtained from the barrows on the sea front during the day.

The beach was one of the stoniest I've ever seen, and very poor for bathing. If the sea didn't appear, there was interest for some in the derelict cement works close by. Walks were really excellent in both directions: fascinating cliffs to explore, partly wooded westwards, and crumbling limestone to the east, with a fossil-hunter's paradise on the beach below.

If there was any hostility to Summerhill from the locals, I don't recall it. The school at one time put on a production for the town, something well-known, possibly *Much Ado About Nothing* or *The Farmer's Wife*.

Neill adopted a characteristic low profile. He could usually be found in his workshop or tinkering with his car. At this time he was addicted to beating sheet brass into ashtrays and similar articles, a craze which seemed to take a long time to pass. He was quite frequently visited by intellectual friends. Among these I particularly remember the writer Ethel Mannin, and a delightful couple, Eric and Doris Dingwall. Professor Dingwall was the official investigator of the Society for Psychical Research, which he combined with a passion for beachcombing.

Mrs Lins [Lilian Neustatter] was very intelligent, warm-hearted and motherly. Although strong-willed she seemed the perfect partner for Neill. I think she was in her element at Lyme, probably happier with a brood of modest size than later on in Leiston. She often used to read to some of us in the sitting room, a nice habit that did not end after Lyme. She was a most accomplished tennis player and together with her son Wally, who became a frequent visitor, formed the core of the school's tennis elite.

Corky, or Corks as he was inevitably called, was a very significant figure. Being chemistry teacher was only a small part of his achievements and qualities. He was unobtrusive, yet able to generate interest in all manner of things. I don't like the description leader – he was different from that – but he arranged numerous excursions, including two in-term camps and two continental expeditions to France and Germany in the holidays. He was perfect at this, and nothing serious ever went wrong. He was also a great companion, with his own brand of quiet Yorkshire humour. He was Neill's right-hand man. I don't know if Neill realised just how lucky he was to have him at Summerhill.

Jonesie was very much the academic and intellectual. Try as I would, I could not see her as anything but extremely plain to look at; but this was amply compensated by her sincerity and warmth. She was second only to George Corkhill as the longest-serving member of staff. I doubt if it was her fault I didn't thrive in her maths class.

At autumn term 1927 we were off to Leiston – Lyme quickly taking its place in the store of memories. Hardly a look back, there was so much excitement over the new house and surroundings: a new world to explore. I suppose at the time of arrival at Leiston the number of pupils, with new additions that term, had grown to around 20 or 25, and it didn't stop there.

I was at Leiston and associated with it for a great many years longer than Lyme. In all that time I have become very familiar with its character, and grown to like it. I have no nostalgia whatever for Lyme Regis as a place. But I will never forget that it was where, by sheer good fortune, I joined a unique school community which completely changed the course of my life.

I have often been asked what it was like in the early days at Summerhill, whether it has changed and, most importantly, did it feel the same. I can quite confidently say that the unmistakeable feeling and reality of freedom and understanding which exists in Summerhill – or in other words the essential ethos of its community life – was precisely the same all those years ago as it is today. I doubt whether anyone who understands Summerhill and its principles will need to ask why this is so.

This chapter is based on an article by Brian Anscombe and edited by Albert Lamb and Hussein Lucas. Brian Anscombe was no longer alive when this book was being prepared.

Robert Townshend
1928-33

In 1927 Lilian Neustatter divorced her husband, Otto, and married Neill. Later that year the lease for the house on "Summer Hill" ran out and after a short tour they found new premises for the school in Leiston, Suffolk, taking the name Summerhill with them. Apart from the war years, when the school evacuated to Wales, this has remained the home of Summerhill ever since.

The widespread idea that Summerhillians are all from liberal or left-wing backgrounds is belied by Robert Townshend. His father was an officer in the regular army and Robert had been sent to a prep school prior to his arrival at Summerhill. The influence of Summerhill was to lead him to a successful and fulfilling career very far removed from what one might have expected from someone of his background and class.

Robert Townshend was born in 1917 in Regent's Park, London. In the 1920s his father was stationed in Ireland where Robert attended day and boarding schools before being sent on to preparatory school in Kent to join his brother, Pat, who was three and a half years older. "It was a very orthodox, strict school," Robert recalled. "You know, the usual thing, the staff made life easy for themselves by creating an atmosphere of fear. You could get sent to the headmaster's study to be caned for absolutely trivial offences like talking in the dormitory."
Not surprisingly neither of the two brothers was happy in this environment. "One term, Pat – rather courageously I think – simply refused to go back there." This was in 1926. "It so happened that my rather brilliant and freethinking Uncle Frank, who spent most of his life abroad, happened to be in England and my mother said, 'Oh, Frank, do please see if you can find another school for Pat.' So Uncle Frank looked into it in a kind of scientific way, trenching through what were the progressive schools, and eventually came up with Summerhill which at that time was in Lyme Regis."
Robert asked his mother if he could also leave the school, but instead of sending him to Summerhill she sent him initially to another

preparatory school. "This was rather of the same ilk as my previous school and the headmaster was in some ways even more pathological. The joke was his name was Evill." Robert was there for a year. "Of course, I saw Pat during the holidays and he painted an absolutely delightful picture of Summerhill; so I asked if I could go there instead and, possibly a bit reluctantly, my parents agreed." This was in 1928 shortly after the school had moved to Leiston. Robert found the freedom at Summerhill astonishing – "Utterly unlike any school I've ever met, probably because it was all compulsion in ordinary schools. Always was and still is. I'd never realised that schools needn't be oppressive. I felt completely free and thrived there."

Robert remembers reading a fair bit and doing a lot of practical activities such as making radio sets and doing up bikes. Skills such as soft-soldering were picked up from older pupils. He had discovered he liked woodwork at prep school, although the amount of time given over to it was trifling. But at Summerhill, although there was no serious woodwork teaching, there was unlimited access to a workshop.

He was also very interested in his surroundings – objects and in particular furniture. "My housemother was Lucy Francis, who later went on to found her own school, and her sitting room with its Georgian furniture and paintings was a big influence."

Pupils came from very varied backgrounds and nationalities. Sweden was strongly represented at that time. Some parents sent their children there because they were in favour of Neill's methods, others because the kids were having problems. Robert remembers some pupils who were perhaps a little bit subnormal in some way, one in particular who seemed more like a man than a pupil. "There were others from the middle or upper-middle classes who had come unstuck in orthodox education, as really my brother and I had. Neill was always very discreet about people's reasons for coming to Summerhill. Rather like a doctor who doesn't discuss his patients' problems."

However, most of the pupils themselves were pretty open about their pasts. Many children went through a destructive phase and there was often a lot of thieving. "Neill instinctively realised that coming down on it like a ton of bricks wasn't a good idea. He believed that somehow or other people would live through it if they were treated decently. If someone got caught swiping something, probably the meeting would say, Oh, well, he must be fined a proportion of his pocket money until this has been paid back. It was purely practical without any heavy moral overtones. The meetings were a very pleasant way of keeping cohesion in the community."

Having been to all-boys schools and not having any sisters it was delightful to mix with the opposite sex. "I think that sexual attraction and appreciation of looks happens very early on and I feel that Summerhill helped me to develop a healthy attitude towards the opposite sex. Pubescent boys are often a bit afraid of girls, and that's probably why they pull their legs a bit. It's just defensive. But Summerhill was the most natural way of gradually developing a reasonable attitude to girls and feeling at ease with them. Marvellous."

As regards the traditional business of schools, Robert feels that Neill may have erred a bit too much in the direction of neglect. "He obviously didn't believe in forcing people to learn, but I think he was a bit neurotic about it. If people don't learn to read and write they're actually handicapped, and there's no point in turning somebody out from a school if they're handicapped. If you love someone you want to make them strong enough to cope with the world, and obviously a certain amount of learning is necessary. You can do it in the most pleasant way – learning shouldn't be punishment like it is in orthodox schools. But I think if people are not gently taken in hand and taught to read by a certain age then it is not freedom it is neglect. Fortunately some members of staff realised this and took it upon themselves to give a bit of extra coaching."

After a year at Summerhill Robert, whose then ambition was to go into the navy, asked his parents if he might transfer to a day school. "I thought that probably I wasn't going to do enough work at Summerhill, simply because it wasn't compulsory." He went to St. Paul's prep school in London where he began to have doubts about his ambition to become a naval officer. A medical check-up showed that his left eye was very astigmatic. "So I wouldn't have got into Dartmouth

Naval Officers School anyway – much to my relief." He returned to Summerhill.

Both Robert's parents got on well with Neill, "though they probably felt it was a bit of a failure for Pat and me to go to Summerhill, whereas Uncle Frank had enough wit to understand it much more, sort of in the round."

When he was 14 Robert's mother died. His father had recently retired from the army and was running a hotel in London. "That wasn't much of a home for me, so in a way Summerhill became my home, certainly from an emotional point of view." This was to remain the case for several years after Robert had left. "I was a regular visitor there for quite a long time afterwards, before starting my own family and making friends in connection with my profession. It was a lovely influence."

Robert recalls Summerhill as being an organised, lively place in those days, with twice-weekly hockey games, including away matches, long cycling expeditions on Sundays, twice-weekly visits to the cinema and plenty of drama with plays usually written by Neill or the children. There was also a magazine, *The Summerhill Joker*, which Robert would sometimes assist with after he'd left school.

At that time Neill was still holding his Private Lessons – psychological therapy for both children and adults – although Robert never attended these. "But we had some jolly good informal chats. I liked him, but I think he was really rather a shy man. He kind of protected himself with rather abstruse jokes. He would try to say something that was almost quizzically unfathomable. It was his way of making friends with you."

Robert feels that Neill's ambivalence about teaching was perhaps inevitable. "It was some kind of hang-up with him. But on the other hand, unless Neill had had hang-ups he probably never would have started Summerhill. So if I've got any small carpings it's simply that people aren't God and the best people have got human errors. I couldn't over emphasise that I look upon it as a major piece of good fortune that I went to Summerhill and came under Neill's influence."

Robert remembers Mrs Lins as being a very good influence, though very different from Neill. "She was more orthodox than he was, but some of her orthodox virtues were really very good for the school. For instance, she had what some people might think of as a sort of bourgeois wish to have things looking nice and tidy and in good order. The house and grounds were always well cared for. It had originally been the home of the heads of the Garrett's works in Leiston, built in either Edwardian or late-Victorian times, with the kind of garden and grounds to go with that period. There were two grass tennis courts and a gravel path with pleasant trees around it. There was this Victorian preoccupation with specimen trees, so an observant boy or girl could go round and see one of all sorts of trees: walnut trees, a magnificent beech – called the Big Beech – variegated conifers and an exceptionally beautiful specimen of the sequoia family from China with very feathery leaves. It's still there on the left as you come down the drive. There was a paid gardener and all the school's vegetables were grown on the spot. Mrs Lins kept this in the same sort of order in which she'd inherited it."

Mrs Lins' sitting-room was a favourite place for informal evening gatherings where she would preside over a sort of salon-like atmosphere. "Inevitably a lot of the rooms were fairly spartan, and for anyone with any aesthetic feeling, even though they might not be conscious of it, going into a civilised room was a nourishing thing." She did have a conventional side to her. "I feel that she was perhaps residually a little bit snobbish, though in a perfectly harmless way." This came out in her attitude towards parents. "Probably she would be a bit more pleased to have a member of the poshocracy."

In sexual matters too she was rather more restrained. "One evening I was in one of the girls' rooms having a chat. I was fully clothed and not engaged in anything the least erotic when Mrs Lins looked in and said, 'Bobby, get out at once, this is a school not a bordello.' I was delighted with this because I've always loved words and I thought bordello was a choice word. I'd never heard it before."

It was through Mrs Lins that Robert came to make his first piece of furniture. "I got my pocket money by the month and I realised I was going to run out unless I did something. I noticed that the sofa in the staff room was on its last legs so I went to Mrs Lins and said, 'I'll make you a new sofa for the staff room, if you like.' And she said, 'Oh, all right, go ahead.' So my month's pocket money – a fiver or whatever it was – I invested in raw materials. I designed it as a very substantial piece. I had to pioneer it, nobody had taught me upholstery or anything, but it turned out to be properly made. I thought it only reasonable to leave Mrs Lins to choose the covering material, so we went to the local shop. Mrs Lins wanted the cheapest stuff but I saw some that I actually liked, that was only a little more expensive. I had a bit of a confrontation with Mrs Lins in the shop and ended up saying, 'Well, if I can't have this better stuff I'll sell my sofa to someone else.' Anyway, she gave way and the funny thing was she ended up liking the sofa so much that she had it in her room and left the staff with the old one." Unfortunately this pioneering work no longer exists. "It disappeared during the war. Maybe it got chopped up for firewood."

After Summerhill

I left Summerhill without formal qualifications and with no idea what to do. My father said, 'You're sixteen, isn't it about time you thought of a career?' I didn't know what to do but, because I was one of those mechanically-minded boys who used to make their own radio sets, electrical engineering was just the first thing that occurred to me. I felt a bit under pressure to make some preparation for earning a living. I started an electrical engineering course at Faraday House but I came unstuck. I was not really good enough at maths for one thing. Also I suppose you could say I've got an artistic temperament – if that doesn't sound too pretentious. I find it very difficult to bring my intelligence to bear on something that doesn't excite my imagination. So during the third year of this four-year course I dropped out.

Summerhill had given me a different way of looking at things from most people. It did give one a very different orientation about progressive views, I suppose. There were subjects that one tended to keep off a bit, because one thought that they were conventional, or maybe even dubious or salacious. But in the course of one's life you simply learn to twig and adjust, and try not to drop bricks.

I continued to visit Summerhill at weekends, often staying with May Chadwick the art mistress who had built a house nearby. She took a sort of motherly interest in me. So quite often when I came down I would stay in her attic. I'd pay something, and probably I had my meals at Summerhill and would settle up with Mrs Lins. I think Summerhill had a dance on Sunday as well as Saturday night, so I used to get up fiendishly early on Monday morning and motor back to London to get to Faraday House in time for the nine o'clock lecture. I was probably at Summerhill more weekends than I wasn't. Even during the war when Summerhill was in Ffestiniog, I used to visit sometimes when I was on leave.

When I was 21 I came into some money. So theoretically I could do anything or nothing. This wonderful uncle of mine happened to be in England again and I was saying, 'Somehow I feel something to do with art or crafts is what I want,' and he took me round to several art schools. We went to Chelsea, and that seemed to me to be very much fine art which I wasn't interested in, and then we went to the Central School of Arts & Crafts in Southampton Row. My uncle and I and the principal of the School of Furniture and Interior Decoration – a rather benign architect called J. C. Rogers – sat down to discuss things. And after a while he said to me, 'If you'd like to, do join us,' even though I hadn't got any written qualifications. It was one of the kind things that sometimes happen to you that you remember. So I went to the Central and found I was very interested in learning cabinet-making.

Here I found I had reasonable gifts and could get on all right. The Central was fairly good for me in that it whetted my appetite and at the same time restored my self-confidence that I could succeed at something. Anyway, 1938 was a bad year to start any sort of course because the following year war broke out.

I wasn't surprised. The Munich crisis was about a year before, so nobody had any excuses for not realising that horrid things were in the offing. I didn't relish the idea of going into the ranks, not entirely from snobbish reasons; I realised that the discipline was completely autocratic, that one was more of a thing than a person. My attitude to authority was certainly coloured by Summerhill. I didn't take authority seriously. I tended to think of those people as power-drunk Pooh-Bahs. I wasn't intimidated by them in the sense that I was overawed by them and thought they were nature's marvels. I only have respect for how people wield necessary authority for some common good.

It so happened that another Old Summerhillian, Brian Anscombe, had had some employment as a radio officer in merchant ships. So both Roger Anscombe [Brian's elder brother] and I suddenly thought, 'Why don't we do this?' We trained at the British School of Telegraphy, got our certificates, and both went to sea in about May 1940. Our employers were the Marconi Company. The training was private but of course it fell into the category of reserved occupation. I was never exactly a fire-eater, but I thought it was proper that Hitler and the Nazis shouldn't succeed. And the idea of death didn't seem so ghastly at the time as the idea of oppressive discipline. Subsequently I learned that the Merchant Navy had a higher casualty rate than any of the armed forces. Apparently one in four was killed.

Apart from occasional shore leave, and an extended spot of sick leave, I spent the rest of the war at sea. I took part in the Atlantic convoys as well as sailing to India, Australia, Africa and elsewhere. I was also in a famous convoy called JW51B, which was taking ammunition to Murmansk in Russia, and was later the subject of a chapter in a book called *Ordeal Below Zero* by George Blond. The Germans knew about the convoy. The Hipper and some other German cruiser were supposed to ambush us, but their ambush went slightly wrong. They didn't converge at exactly the same moment and so our escort, which was six destroyers, very gallantly fought off the Hipper. Thanks to them our entire escort got to Murmansk unscathed. When we'd unloaded our supplies and were on the way home I asked the mate exactly what the cargo had consisted of. He said, 'Well, it was mostly ammunition, but there were also some Red Cross supplies and cocoa...and 200 tons of TNT.' So I was jolly glad to get home.

Other convoys I was on turned out to be not quite so hazardous. No ship that I was on was ever hit and quite often the convoys were not attacked. There's no question that I was extremely lucky.

Towards the end of the war the Allies gained mastery of the air and the U-boat menace was considerably reduced with the invention of Asdic. I don't remember experiencing much fear. I was frightened of perceived dangers, such as on the Russian trip, but one had to go through with it and hope for the best. And on the whole it was quite interesting. But really – this sounds selfish when one considers what happened to people on the continent of Europe, particularly the Jews – in my life the war was a blasted nuisance. It interrupted my career and meant that I wasn't able to be with my girlfriend and had to live on rather ghastly food. I think probably most English people who were in the war felt that it was simply a nasty job that had to be done, even though it was a damned nuisance doing it. There wasn't any kind of flag-waving.

In 1941 I was in the Kingston Clinic in Edinburgh, being treated for sinus trouble, and it was there I met my future wife, Eva, who was visiting her sister. Neill was indirectly responsible for this as the sisters' cousin had visited Summerhill and heard about the clinic from him. Neill was a friend of J.C. Thomson, the naturopath who ran the clinic, and he had occasionally stayed there himself. Eva and I were married in 1943.

After the war I wanted to resume my training in furniture, cabinet-making and design and I'd come to realise that the Central probably wasn't the ideal place to learn this. I happened to be in Shearns vegetarian restaurant when a Summerhill parent came in. I told her I was looking for somewhere to learn about furniture design and cabinet-making and she said 'Oh, you must go to Edward Barnsley who lives at Froxfield in Hampshire.' So I went down and enrolled as a paying pupil at £80 a year. Although I didn't really like Edward Barnsley's furniture that much – if he had been a designer in the classical tradition I would have been that much happier – I was given an excellent training. There were first-rate cabinet-makers there and the work was very well organised. One learnt the whole process from scale-drawings to the final wax polish. It was a lovely place to learn. I stayed there for two and a half years, then I bought this house not far from Leiston and set up my workshop in one of the rooms, where I've worked ever since.

The classical influence in my work comes principally from observation, from looking at furniture. I was always interested in the appearance of things. Visual images. In order to promote my work I enrolled in various societies such as the Arts & Crafts Exhibition Society and the Craft Centre of Great Britain where I was able to exhibit all the year round. People would either buy these things, and the Craft Centre would take a commission, or someone would like your style but want another article, so you would get work like that. Then a very good thing happened. In about 1970, Suffolk Crafts Society was formed. I was a founder member. They provided us with somewhere to exhibit at Snape Maltings, and we held exhibitions during the Aldeburgh Festival. So cultured persons with long purses came down, and from my point of view it was miles better than anything the London societies could do. And I never looked back.

I doubt very much whether I could have survived and brought up a family purely on my earnings. I relied on my private income. That dwindled and then as luck would have it various relatives died and left me a bit more. So I've been very lucky post-war. I've never had to do anything other than what I wanted by way of occupation.

I took up a teaching post for a while in Ipswich Civic College, more as a challenge, to see whether I could cope with it, although the pay was approximately three times as much per hour as I could earn on my own. I found that creative manual work was looked down upon: it was thought suitable for people who are a bit witless, almost a therapy for nutcases. I thought that that attitude is absolutely preposterous. 'O' level economic history for example is something you can simply mug up and squirt out, whereas my work requires imagination and different kinds of wit. It hardly helped me if the boys in my class thought they were in some kind of bin. So I began to despise the attitude of orthodox education. I didn't really enjoy teaching, though I stuck it for two years in order not to abandon the boys midstream. Keeping people in order and behaving like a policeman is not my attitude to cabinet-making. If people want to be a blasted nuisance and fool about, they shouldn't be there. But orthodox education isn't like that. You've got to be there. In other words teaching volunteers is an entirely different kettle of fish to teaching conscripts. But I did the best I could and there weren't any serious contretemps. A reasonable percentage of my pupils passed the exam, though there was one disappointment. One boy, who I thought was easily the most gifted of the lot, actually failed. Then I learnt afterwards that during the exam his parents were in the middle of a divorce. So that's the sort of thing people are up against. One of life's little bits of bad luck.

Since then I've worked on my own, and always had enough to keep me going. If I hadn't got any orders, then I would make something on spec to put into an exhibition. People seem to find my work sufficiently useful and charming for them to buy it, so I don't have things on my hands. I don't know whether my work is original. Originality is really rather a funny word to conjure with. There's a sort of post-war feeling that the amount of originality is directly linked to the worth of the object itself. This is what I would call originality fever. As far as the useful arts are concerned, Terence Conran said that if a thing doesn't work it's not a good design. So for instance, there was a vogue at one time among the potters for a rather tall beaker with a round handle at the bottom of it. That was original but the thing was top-heavy and needed ten times as much muscle to keep it upright, so it was just damn silly. Individuality is something else. I feel that most collectors would recognise my work. I tend to shun publicity. I have been written about, but I rather naively believe that one's work ought to speak for itself.

I've got three grown-up sons. I hope I haven't been authoritarian as a parent but I do feel there has to be a balance in the upbringing of children. You have to have enough authority to stop anything really foolish happening which they can't see the consequences of. I certainly don't believe in the way some of the young now bring up children, so that they can actually be free to be antisocial. In other words the brattish or egocentric behaviour that one sometimes sees. As Neill said, freedom has its limits when we are treading on the freedom of others. And bringing up kids is precisely the same idea.

I obviously hadn't enough money to send three kids to boarding school. Also, after the war attitudes to education were changing. When I was young you would be looked upon as a failure by your class if your children had to go to council schools. I did send my eldest son to Summerhill for a time, but I found Neill's attitude to me as a parent rather cold and distant, which was rather off-putting, though later we got on perfectly well again. I think Neill had an unresolved hang-up about his parents, so therefore parents had an emotional symbolism for him. Also Summerhill seemed to have rather less organisation than it had had when I was a pupil. So I sent him to New Sherwood. It seemed to me at the time to be rather more realistic. It had all the advantages of a friendly atmosphere and no repression, but I think they probably concentrated a bit more on having more organised games and activities. In other words there was slightly less drift. I thought it had a more purposeful air.

My second son went to Leiston Grammar and the youngest to the Secondary Modern. As with most families the relationship between father and sons became strained for a time as they grew up. I'm glad I've lived as long as I have because you can come to terms with your children's criticism. Nowadays we get on perfectly well. I've come to realise that when kids grow up they have to make this transition of leaving home and going out into the outside world. So, they have to kick themselves out of the nest and their parents are part of the nest. And therefore the parents get kicked. If you get kicked that's tough. But if you have kids that's a part of it. That has to be gone through. You have to understand it and simply bear it as best you can, and try and smooth things over later.

I feel I have maintained a good disposition throughout my life. Obviously one has had bad patches, but on the whole I think I'm reasonably happy and outgoing. Constructive I think is a good word. I can't remember ever feeling bored. It's too easy to find things to do. My health has been very good. I think there is a strong connection between emotional and physical health. People use themselves up with tension. It's all energy which might go towards being constructive, even if it's only being nice to other people. I've always liked exercise; I go swimming and I've always liked living in the country, so I've had fresh air. I did smoke at one time, but never terribly heavily like my brother did. I think I have always had a natural instinct to try and be healthy.

I've never adhered to any belief system, whether communism or anything else. I feel sure that the more fulfilled a person's life is all round, with their finding an outlet for their own talents and being able to do that, the less one needs a belief, which I think is just some rather pathetic comfort that some people need. Insofar as a person's life continues after death, I feel that this is simply a genetic continuation, and whether any influence I've had on my children and friends and acquaintances has made any difference to their lives – and such of my artefacts as survive. It's very vague. But I think once you're dead that's it.

My wife died some years ago. I feel it was a successful marriage. I think people have to be exceptionally decent and I would say have an exceptionally mature attitude to have a reasonable marriage. I mean they have to have a kind of unwritten pact that they are going to be faithful to each other, otherwise things can bust up. Once people start going off in different directions it can cause tension. And they must treat each other reasonably decently because they are actually trapped with each other. There may be some modern people who think it doesn't matter, that children don't mind and it isn't going to do them any harm if their parents' marriages bust up, but I was never one to think like that. I thought it important to try to get on.

I do feel that society is in a state of decline. I think it's absolutely frightening really. If Marx was right about anything, he was right about saying – if I'm quoting him correctly – that quantitative change leads to qualitative change. You can just simply look at something like the amount of car exhaust fumes that are belched forth in England. Maybe in the 1920s there was little enough of it for the atmosphere to take and absorb. Now it's a problem. Farming provides another example. When we first came here they had a rather labour-intensive way of killing weeds with harrowing. Nowadays there's all that silliness of modern farming methods with its chemical fertilisers. So these are just two simple examples of the way in which the world is being flagrantly abused, quite apart from CFCs.

You could almost say the world is divided up into people who take a long-term view and those who take a short-term view. And the short-termists always get their own way until somebody prevents them. There are so many people who think that it's clever to make a quick buck and to hell with what's happening. So I'm horrified about that. I'm also horrified of course about the potency of destructive weapons. It only needs some tinpot dictator whom some unscrupulous person has sold some plutonium and what-not to suddenly upset the whole works. So I think the world's a very frightening place and I feel very sorry for the young who are growing up with all these rather horrid prospects.

Whatever minor criticisms I may make about Summerhill, I have no doubt that these are outweighed by its positive qualities. The wonderful thing about Summerhill was that it acted as a sort of bridge between schooldays and finally growing up and becoming independent. In other words, Summerhill doesn't stop when you stop being a pupil. I was obviously dependent on it for several years after I'd left. But then you're dependent on society, and Summerhill was more than a school. It was like a family of old friends and acquaintances. All in all, I think I owe Neill and his creation a great debt.

Postscript (2011)

Robert has now retired from furniture making. He still enjoys doing crossword puzzles.

Mike Bernal
1932-40

In the 1930s many left-wing and liberal parents began sending their children to Summerhill, not as a last resort, but because they believed in Neill's ideas. There is an assumption one often encounters that Summerhill with its philosophy of free development must be an unsuitable environment for people of strong intellectual potential. In spite of the evidence that many successful people do not find their vocation until later in life, the tendency in mainstream education to force-feed pupils in certain disciplines runs counter to this recognition.

Mike Bernal came from a distinguished scientific background, and was to make his own mark in that field. However, he did not show any particular interest in science and maths until he had left school, preferring to spend his time in the art room or participating in the rich social life of the community.

Mike Bernal was born in 1926. His father, J.D. Bernal, popularly known as 'Sage', was a physicist at Cambridge University who was very well known in his time, not only for his scientific work – he was a pioneer in crystallography – but also as a Marxist and as someone who attempted to build bridges during the cold war period. He wrote several books of which the best known are probably *The World, the Flesh and the Devil* and *The Social Function of Science*. Mike's mother had worked for the economist John Maynard Keynes and was very involved in the Peace Movement in the inter-war years.

Mike has no idea how his parents heard of Summerhill. "But at any rate they sent both myself and later my brother Egan there." Prior to that Mike had been to a little nursery school in Cambridge which, as far as he remembers, he enjoyed. He was six when he went to Summerhill. "I loved it, right from the beginning. I can't remember any time that I was unhappy." Although Mike was very fond of his parents, particularly his mother, he didn't find it difficult leaving them, even at such a young age. "In fact," Mike recalls, "it was rather nice, because I loved going down to Summerhill and at the end of

53

term I liked coming back home. So I had the best of both worlds."

From Mike's point of view almost all the staff were wonderful. "One or two almost like heroes." Lessons, however, did not occupy much of the day. "We did go to them, and for the most part we enjoyed them, but otherwise we mucked around – cycling, climbing trees, building huts. It was an absolutely marvellous playground for children. I can't remember any serious accidents although some of the trees we climbed were enormous. But there was nobody to say, don't do that."

Everyone got on pretty well socially, Mike recalls. "There were gangs of a kind, but not in the sense that they were trying to do anything to anybody else. There was a sense of adventure." He remembers raiding the larder with one of his mates. "We got caught and were outlawed for a little while." The General Meetings were very good at making up the school rules and making decisions about anybody breaking them. "There was always the understanding that if people behaved in an anti-social fashion it was very largely due to the fact that they were missing out on love of one kind or another. Quite seriously. That was the way we felt about it. And one appreciated that from quite a young age."

Mike is certain that Summerhill was a genuine democracy. "This idea of the democratic resolution of problems that one picked up from the General Meetings was a powerful influence, even though they occupied a very small part of one's time."

Plays and dramatic improvisations, known at Summerhill as 'spontaneous acting', were also an important influence. "You were able to explore other people's points of view and also get up and express your own." End-of-term plays were a highlight. "A lot of work went into producing and writing them. I enjoyed acting."

Mike can't recall reading a lot. "I guess I read all the kids' magazines like *The Hotspur* and *Film Fun* and I would certainly go every week to the cinema." There were dances every weekend in the lounge. "I have a nice memory sometimes of a summer evening when the sun has set and the light coming from the lounge…that light coming…it's a lovely kind of memory at the back of my mind. And the music…the noise of the music sort of floating out. Great stuff."

Mike was a little in awe of Neill when he first met him. "But I thought he was a wonderful guy and I still do. There are very few people I can say that about. He was absolutely remarkable; really incredible." Neill would tell stories to the younger children, which he made up as he went along, in which they became characters. He eventually wrote these up into a couple of books. Mike appears in *The Last Man Alive.*

Mike doesn't remember Neill as a teacher. "What I do remember is that the lessons I went to I enjoyed, and I was never put off anything. So I think it stood me in good stead for the rest of my life. The important thing is that everything was voluntary." He found Mrs Lins a bit remote. "One stood in awe of her. As far as anything was strict in Summerhill, she was."

Mike particularly enjoyed arts and crafts and seriously considered whether he should try to be an artist when he left school. He concluded, "Well, if I'm a scientist I can always do art on the side. Of course it didn't work out like that, but it was that close because we had various artistic people around who obviously influenced me a lot. In the event, once I'd left Summerhill I don't suppose I ever did anything artistic again."

He was an enthusiastic sportsman. "I played cricket, football, hockey. I was very good at sprinting. There would be something like a sports day, but I don't think it was laid on in the sense of people taking it too seriously." He remembers that the girls joined in most things and the relationship between the sexes was pretty equal. "Though the girls probably tended to keep something to themselves and the boys equally something to themselves. There were a lot of romances of one kind or another going on. It was wonderful."

During the civil war in Spain there was an influx of Spanish girls. "I think they made a big impact. They were very beautiful girls. Sonia Araquistain, who I think was the daughter of the Spanish ambassador, or at any rate a high-ranking official, and another girl who particularly sticks in my mind. I guess I thought all girls were beautiful then, but they were unusual. They were older than I was, so I don't think there was any question of any romance."

After the outbreak of war, when the school moved to Ffestiniog, Mike went with it, but for one term only. "By then a lot of the really good teaching staff had left, been called up and one thing and another, and I thought, if I'm going to do anything I'd better find something else."

After Summerhill

I found a nice old guy in Cambridge who coached me in physics and chemistry for about a year, and then I went to the Battersea Polytechnic in 1941, now Surrey University, I think. The teachers there were absolutely brilliant, so any interest I'd had in physics, and to a lesser extent in chemistry and mathematics, was certainly reinforced there.

The war was on and I remember I felt I should do something. So, because I was still studying, I joined the Air Training Corps. And I was an air raid messenger. I guess one felt one was on the right side and one needed to do these things. Our house was never hit but one remembers very well the noise, the bombs exploding in the distance.

I think I was almost entirely in my parents' house during the war years. My father was assessing bomb damage and then later on he worked for Lord Mountbatten as a scientific adviser in a thing called Combined Operations. One of the things he did was to assess the possibility of landing craft on the French shore. Whether he went there before the D-Day landing I don't know. But he was fearless, there's no doubt about that.

I did my Matric and Intermediate at Battersea and then in 1943 I went to Imperial College, London, to the Mathematics Department. In 1945 I got my BSc with first-class honours. Then, because I was still eligible for call-up, I joined the Department of Chemical Technology at Imperial.

Most people say they can remember what they were doing when Kennedy was assassinated. I think I can remember when I heard the news that the atomic bomb had been dropped. I was at a friend's house in the country, and I arrived to find everybody was out, and I put the radio on and there was this incredible piece of news. I think there were two things I thought about it. One was it meant the ending of the war. The other was that I naively thought that if this energy could be tapped, then the world would solve its energy problems, and hopefully solve many other problems at the same time. I now see of course that things are never quite as simple as that. Later on I took part in the CND demonstrations, but this business of whether or not nuclear energy could be used to provide the world with energy, I just don't know. I'd be delighted if it could in some ways.

While I was at Imperial I went to a lecture given by a guy called Frank Boys on theoretical chemistry, and I was so taken with this that I decided to do my PhD. He was a marvellous supervisor, so I was very lucky. I did my PhD in mathematical physics, I suppose you'd call it, which I must have finished in 49/50. Then I became a research assistant to Professor Massey at University College. Massey was a very distinguished, brilliant mathematician and physicist, so I was very lucky there. When that piece of work was done I went to Queen Mary College and taught, surprisingly, in the Physics Department – because I hadn't got a degree in physics. Then I moved to the Physics Department at King's College, and it happened to be the time when all the fundamental work on DNA was being done. So I got to know a lot of those people like Maurice Wilkins, but, regrettably not, Rosalind Franklin. It was an exciting time.

While I was there somebody had arranged for a series of lectures to be given on computers. Two of my mates at Imperial had been developing a computer; I think they were unaware of the things that were going on in places like Bletchley Park, but they were very good. So I'd been caught up a little bit in this computer world, and at King's this continued. And when an ad came up for an appointment to the University of London Computer Unit, as it was going to be called, I applied for it and got it. That was in 1958. At that time computers were incredibly expensive and enormous. Occupied a wall. I gave courses in programming. In those days the programming languages were incredibly primitive. As time went on of course they got more sophisticated. I got my readership in mathematics in 1969, and stayed there until 1974, by which time almost all the colleges had begun to buy computers and the Institute of Computer Science, as it had become, no longer had any particular function.

So I was without a job. A little bit worrying. Then I had an offer from University College to join the Mathematics Department there, and also one from Imperial, and the people in Imperial seemed rather more enthusiastic so I accepted, and I've been there since. In fact I retired a few years ago but stayed on as a consultant. I'm now an Emeritus Reader.

I think how incredibly lucky it is to get paid for something one enjoys doing. One can't complain. I'm sure that everybody has times in their lives when things go badly, and I've had some pretty dreadful times, but basically I've been very lucky.

I guess in a sense I was always left-wing in my politics. Probably a bit naive. Even as a child, because I was aware of all the dreadful things that were happening all over the world. One didn't have to know much about fascism to know that it was a dreadful thing. So those who resisted it seemed to be the good guys. I remember seeing Russian films and they were very inspiring. I can understand why I was caught up and perhaps didn't see that although there were some very good things going on in Russia there were also some very dreadful things.

I wouldn't have said the whole of Summerhill was political at that time, but there were some of us whose families had socialistic backgrounds. By the time the war came of course the idea of being anti-fascist, anti-Nazi was general. I think David Barton was like myself; his mother, Jonesie, was, I'm sure. His father had been an explorer and vanished, so I don't know what his father's political affiliations were. I'm pretty certain that Leslie Morton was very left-wing.

I joined the Communist Party at the time of the height of McCarthyism because I was so appalled at what was going on in countries like the US. It's awfully difficult to say, but I think there was a near-fascist element there. I guess I stayed a member for a good

58

few years; then, I suppose, like many people became disillusioned; not with the ideals at all, the ideals of communism always seemed to be fine, but with Stalinism. I think, regarding the show trials, I probably kidded myself that the accused really were guilty, but then realised that it was the accusers who were the guilty ones. As time goes on you can't ignore that kind of thing. I didn't have a big break, I just quit. There were marvellous people in the CP, good people who unfortunately hadn't seen through Stalinism.

Since then I've been fairly solid Labour. The Labour Party's been through some horrendous times and I think the Thatcher years were disastrous on the whole, but even so I think it could be argued that some of the things she did could in fact be seen as beneficial. I find it difficult to say that.

I tend to be optimistic about the world. I think in my own time it already has become a better place. I think because of the ending of the cold war the world is a safer place. I must say it heartened me enormously. You have frightening things at the moment in countries like Iraq and so on, but at least if the two major powers are not squabbling too much there's a chance that one can do something to sort these problems out. But again, things are not as easy as all that, with oil interests and one thing and another, and corruption is endemic. There's no particular country has got a monopoly on it.

The ideals of communism still seem to me to be perfectly sensible and good. That people should work together; and nobody should own things while others were dispossessed and so on, I couldn't see the merit in that. And I think the idea of treating everybody as equals makes a lot of good sense. But in the long run it's so difficult to tell, and that's why I think that freedom of the press, freedom of unions and the like, are just so important. There should always be the possibility of dissent.

Thank goodness, there have always been troublemakers around; people who are willing to stand up and be counted. And I'm very lucky to have met many of them. But equally I've met many who always seemed intimidated and where I can I say to people, "For goodness' sake don't put up with being pushed around." Just a tiny example: when I did my undergraduate degree most of the lecturers were very good, but we had one who was absolutely hopeless. So we went to see the head of department and said, "This lecturer's just not doing a good job," and he was taken off from teaching us. I wish people would do that more often.

As far as my own attitude to students is concerned, I hope I treat them just like human beings. With research students you normally develop a fairly close relationship, and I've made some very good friends. If anyone starts being deferential I tell them, "For goodness' sake don't." I'm always a little afraid that they are a bit in awe of us. I try to dispel that as quickly as I can. I'm the departmental careers adviser, so it's very important that I can make them feel they can talk to me just like anyone.

I certainly didn't have any sense of awe about any of my lecturers when I was a student. Of course I had a totally easy relationship with my teachers at Summerhill, and when I went to Battersea Polytechnic the head of the Matric Department was a guy called Dr Waring. He was a delightful guy. In the lunchtimes we used to sit in the lecture room and gossip about absolutely anything. It was no "sir" or anything. So what I mean is there are plenty of people around, thank goodness, who won't accept this nonsense.

I haven't really kept close contact with many Summerhillians. After I left one of the Summerhillians I probably saw most of was someone a bit younger than myself, a guy called Anthony Jenkins who's a very talented photographer. We used to go out drinking together. I've crossed paths with David Barton several times. He became a very distinguished statistician and I might even have suggested that he apply to the Institute of Computer Science. At any rate he applied and was accepted. And later on he had a chair at Queen Mary College, and we would meet at inaugural lectures and occasions like that.

Two or three years ago Branwen Williams invited Tony Oberleitner over for a reunion. It was a great occasion. Seeing people was unbelievable. I don't think I'd seen some of them for about 50 years.

I never have dreamt about Summerhill, and I hardly ever think about it. Fortunately, I've plenty else to think about, though I occasionally think about my old mates. I think when Branwen invited us to see Tony, that was the kind of thing I wouldn't have missed for the world.

I was incredibly lucky to have gone to Summerhill, and I don't seem to have suffered academically because of the fact that it wasn't a traditional school. Quite the reverse I would hope. It may be that anybody who's not been put off subjects wants to go on finding out about the world. I'm sure I'm not unique in this in any way at all. It's forcing people that puts them off. Neill was always seen to be very keen that we shouldn't do Shakespeare for example, because he was afraid – I think quite rightly – that if you did it would put you off.

A lot of one's life is spent doing administration of one kind or another, trying to understand other people, and my experience with a lot of people is that they get tongue-tied. With spontaneous acting you found very early on it didn't matter if you made a fool of yourself. Go ahead and do it. And listening to someone else is part of the Summerhill ethos generally. It's not to believe that anybody has a monopoly on truth. I can't remember chairing any General Meetings, but I've often chaired meetings since and I'm sure the experience I got at Summerhill has been useful. It's this feeling that nothing's too much, "If someone else can do it, why can't I?"

It didn't even cross my mind to send my children to Summerhill, because we thought they'd be living in a loving home, a nice environment, and the other thing you've got to remember of course is that whatever Summerhillians think they've also got to consider what their partner wants.

I didn't keep in touch with Neill after I left. Never visited Summerhill. I would occasionally hear him being interviewed on the radio; I may have seen him on TV once. But whenever I did I was always delighted by what a splendid guy he was. There are very few people one could say that about: the heroes of one's youth who will last into old age. I thought my father was a great guy, though I was probably closer to my mother. I have a lot of good feelings about Churchill. He was just the kind of leader that we needed at the time.

I think he was splendid. And I'm a great admirer of Nelson Mandela. There was a drama the other night about George Best. George Best was the hero. He did in fact appear very briefly at the end, but it was about two young lads who idolised him and wanted to go to a football match in which he was playing. It was lovely, because this was an example of idealising someone who was a real hero. So Neill has always remained a hero. He was a great guy. I'm sceptical, I'm pragmatic and all the rest of it, still at the same time I feel it's very unlikely that there's anything Neill could have said or done that you'd have really said, "Oh, he's not as good as all that."

I think it's not of the greatest importance to me that Summerhill survives. I think it's rather the importance of the ideas...that the ideas can continue and be developed, and people learn from Neill's experience. One hopes that some of the ideas have already been taken up. But at the time it always seemed to me that the success depended a tremendous amount on Neill and his qualities. He was a remarkable person and I always found it difficult to believe anybody would be able to take over after he died. But when I heard Zoë speak at the 70th anniversary – I'd never really met her before – I was delighted. She spoke such good sense and with such warmth and so on, I thought, "Well, OK, she may not be Neill but she doesn't seem to be half bad." So I don't know.

I should say that, if Neill had any message at all, one of them was the idea that love is a very important thing. I don't think anybody really disagrees about that. The other thing was anti-authoritarianism. You shouldn't do anything or think anything simply because you're told to. You should try as well as you can to work things out for yourself. I'm pragmatic, I'm sceptical, and all those things. I try to be scientific. But I think one has to be very open-minded and the like. These were qualities that one gained from Summerhill. I'm appalled what damage is being done to a generation of kids today. It isn't to say that there aren't lots of very good teachers around, but the whole ethos of schools can be incredibly damaging.

I did feel that Neill's influence would spread. Even as a kid I knew that his ideas were influential, as far as many teachers were concerned. But maybe I expected more than actually happened. Summerhill ideas have spread all over the world, but I suspect they are tiny little pockets. On the other hand a lot of other things have happened which I think Neill would have approved of thoroughly. The end of apartheid for example. The idea of liberation. And I think there have been little insidious things, a lot of liberating ideas floating around in films, radio, TV and the world of art, which get into people's homes and make them challenge the accepted authority.

If I look back at the attitude, how people accepted authority in the 30s...now in the 90s I think things are different. People are much more sceptical. I think that working people nowadays won't put up with being treated as dirt.

When I left Summerhill I thought in one sense Summerhillians were better than other people – I can't think of the appropriate word – because Summerhill had perhaps allowed people to free themselves from a lot of hang-ups, hypocrisy and so on. But I now know I was completely wrong. You don't have to be a Summerhillian to be a very good person. There are lots of splendid people all over the world who've never been to Summerhill. Lots of them.

Amongst one's friends one would always notice that somebody was particularly inhibited in some way or another, and one would think poor fellow. But one shared a good deal in the way of common values. On the other hand, when I was a research assistant at University College I became a friend of one of the staff there, a very distinguished sexologist called Alex Comfort. He was a great character. Anyway we must have been talking politics and I was saying I found it difficult to imagine how anybody could be a fascist. And he said, "You sit opposite them every day at lunch." I thought about it afterwards...and you look at what happens in so many countries, how easily so many people can do the most horrific things...and I don't know what the answer is except that one hopes with a more caring world, a better educational system and so on, that we can wholly eradicate that. I think it is to do with love. I find it difficult to believe that anybody who's been brought up in a loving and caring environment, has not been put down or kicked, would ever do anything seriously wrong to their fellow beings.

Postcript (2011)

I have continued to work part-time in my field at the university where I retain a working space. My main interest now is drama. I enjoy being a support worker for my local drama group in Chiswick, dealing with technical matters which mainly involve the use of computers.

Robert Muller
1934-43

Although in the 1930s the balance of the Summerhill intake began to shift from a preponderance of pupils who came because they had experienced problems with the education system, to those who came for more positive reasons, problem children continued to arrive.

As a problem child, having to cope with conflicting parental influences at home, as well as rebelling against authority at school, Robert Muller was to flourish in the free and expansive atmosphere of Summerhill. His innate entrepreneurial instincts were given ample scope to blossom, whilst at the same time his harder edges and combative streak were rounded off and he became an active member of various school committees.

Robert's wife Biddy was also at Summerhill, but for only three years. They met again later in life and married. Biddy was present at the interview and several of her comments and recollections are included.

Robert Muller was born in 1926. Of German descent, his father was a lifelong socialist and a successful businessman who started a firm producing tennis and badminton rackets, "very ably assisted by my mother." The firm originally used synthetic gut racket strings obtained from the German factory owned by another branch of the family. Robert's mother was Jewish, from the Solomon family of matzo bakers in Brick Lane in the East End. "She was very well educated in a practical sense. She was very astute, very intuitive. She always made the right business decisions without being able to explain why. I've come to believe that heredity is much more important than Summerhill and Neill believed in those days." Although from a strongly atheistic background, both at home and at Summerhill, Robert has come to believe that there is a God – "although I'm very anti a paternalistic God with petty ideas. He, she or it can't be as petty as all the religions make him out to be."

Robert went to seven schools before Summerhill and got expelled from most of them. Among these were a Steiner school in Streatham – "high-minded but not practical" - and Dora Russell's school,

Beacon Hill – "which vaguely resembled Summerhill" - with husband Bertrand in attendance. "'Daddy' Russell used to tell us bedtime stories. I was there for a year but don't remember a lot about it. It was my first boarding school and I was only six. I don't think I was particularly happy there." Neill, who knew Russell, felt that he was too intellectual in his approach which had more to do with idealism than instinct. He seems to have approved more of Dora Russell.

After that Robert went to an elementary school, the last before Summerhill. "Because he was a confirmed atheist my father forbade them to give me any religious instruction. I used to get up and go out of class whenever it began. It was accepted. One day I had a dispute with a teacher who tried to prevent me from leaving. 'You'll go when I say so.' I said, 'No, my father has said I am not to have it and so I'm going out.' I was reported to the headmistress for insubordination. She told me she was going to cane me. I remember quite clearly drawing myself up to my full three foot six or whatever it was and saying, 'I feel I ought to tell you, if you try to do that I intend to defend myself.' And I meant it. She then asked my parents to remove me at once."

Robert's father heard of Summerhill through Sol Leff whose son Gordon (known as Bunny) was already there. "My mother, who was a humanist and anti-religion like my father, was enthusiastic. She instinctively liked Neill and felt it was the right thing. It was she who was influential in sending me there and later my younger sister and brother, though my father would certainly have approved." Like many radicals of the time Robert's father saw Summerhill as part of a progressive socialist movement. Indeed, it was expected that Summerhill practice would be absorbed into state education for all once the Labour government got in after the war.

Robert was not enthusiastic at the prospect of going to Summerhill. "I was determined not to like it. I was determined to be unhelpful in any event. I had a strong anti-attitude to anything. I think I must have been the pits. I was the real problem child."

Once there however his attitude quickly changed. "I was thoroughly happy after about a term. I suspect because it was the first time I had been left alone and that was a tremendous relief. Neill's attitude was, 'Oh, well, if you don't want to, bugger off.' I'd been grossly spoilt by my father. My mother was probably trying, quite rightly, to counter this. I never got on with her, something I bitterly regret now. It was probably a relief to get away from both of them. I enjoyed the whole thing."

As with many Summerhillians, Neill was a bit of a background figure, though Robert got to know him better when he began to have Private Lessons, which he found "useful". There were many other adults who made a stronger impression. One of these was Leslie Morton, author of the famous *A People's History of England*, still on the humanities curriculum today. Another adult who taught at Summerhill in the late 1930s was the future clinical psychologist John Graham-White, known to the Summerhill kids as 'Jasper'.

"They were important as people whether as teachers or socially. I never separated lessons and social, and I still don't. It was all part of the same thing."

Before the war, both teachers and parents tended to be academic left-wingers. Although Mike Bernal is almost sure that his father, though a Marxist, was never a member of the Communist Party, several parents and teachers at Summerhill in the 30s certainly were. In those days the discrepancy between educational freedom and the totalitarianism of communism was not so apparent as it later became. Communism and left-wing politics in general tended to be mixed up with pre-war new-ageism in all its variety – the Men's Dress Reform Society, the New Health Society, the World League for Sexual Reform...and Summerhill. Most of the adults at Summerhill at this time, including Neill, would have been perceived as 'bohemians' – pipe-smoking 'lefties' in open-neck shirts and corduroy trousers engaging in nude sunbathing and following 'cranky' diets. Mrs Lins, in charge of the kitchen, ensured a plentiful supply of fresh fruit, raw greens and wholemeal bread – radical at the time – and Neill coined his maxim that of far more importance than the three Rs were the three Fs: freedom, fresh air and fresh food.

"There were a lot of very interesting and intelligent people around. I always went to lessons, certainly after the first couple of terms. The teachers were particularly good at that time, as were the pupils." Robert feels that Summerhill has gone up and down over the years in this respect. For many, the thirties was the golden age of Summerhill. There were certainly a good many high-fliers amongst the pupils, such as Mike Bernal, and David Barton [who became a distinguished physicist], and Gordon Leff who has published several books on Medieval History. His sister, Angela Leff, seemed destined to become a concert pianist but died tragically young of a brain tumour. Michael Boulton (who, Robert remembers, "danced us all off the floor"), became a member of Sadlers Wells Ballet. Robert's younger brother Ralph became a professor of Parasitology and wrote a definitive work on a species of African tapeworm.

"Pupils who transferred from conventional public schools were usually way behind us academically," Robert recalls. This in spite of Neill's public disdain for book learning. "My group in the last years were all very keen on learning. We got rude at Neill and told him we weren't getting adequate preparation for the School Cert. Neill said, 'Oh, you don't want to bother with that,' and we said, 'We bloody well do!' And after that we were properly prepared."

Robert's future wife Biddy grew up in Warwickshire. An only child, her parents sent her at the age of six to a small, coeducational, family-type boarding school which took pupils up to the age of 11. In 1937 she went on to Summerhill and stayed three years, two in Leiston, one in Ffestiniog. Like Robert she found Neill an unobtrusive figure, "but always there if you needed him." She enjoyed Summerhill, "although it could be a bit lonely at times. I was quiet and introspective. I never caused problems and nobody ever gave me any. Summerhill probably does favour more extrovert people simply because it allows you to be more of whatever you are. But I should have liked to have stayed longer." When her parents separated, money became a problem and she had to leave. "In retrospect I would certainly have liked to have stayed longer, especially as a very good art teacher joined shortly after I'd left."

This was Robin Bond under whose tutorship several budding

artists flourished, including Ishbel McWhirter and Evelyn Williams both of whom went on to become successful professional painters.

Although Robert Muller was poor at maths while at Summerhill, he subsequently learned to do accounts when he went into the licensed trade. "I have no affinity for figures but I learned to read accounts not as maths but as a story. A drink and its accessory have a character which is a price that I can visualise very much as I visualise words. And I could add things up. I did go to all the maths lessons at Summerhill, and what I do know about maths is almost certainly down to Neill. I don't know whether you could call him a good maths teacher. I don't suppose Mike Bernal and David Barton would think so, but then they were probably way ahead of him even as kids."

Robert was something of an entrepreneur at Summerhill. "I ran quite a lot of rackets, what Summerhillians referred to as 'swindles'. Various entertainments. I got hold of a cine-projector that I set up in the hut and charged the kids a penny to watch cartoons. My best business was a stamp firm. During the holidays I'd buy sacks of used envelopes with foreign stamps, soak them off in the bath, categorise them with the help of *Stanley Gibbons' Catalogue* and then trade them through adverts in comics like *Hotspur* and *Wizard*. I was making ten bob a week at a time when pocket money was half your age in pence. So I was extremely well-off. I used to reckon that for 6d you could have quite an evening out. The cinema cost 4d and a drink and a bag of chips a penny each."

Robert also produced a school magazine, *The Summerhill Joker*, with pictures and words by staff and pupils. "My father had got me a second-hand Roneo hand-turned printer. I remember being very irate at a General Meeting when someone asked what Robert Muller had to do with *The Summerhill Joker*. I answered in a loud voice: 'I turn the handle!' This was widely quoted at Summerhill for quite a while after."

Sport, cinema, music, dancing, drama and membership of the numerous Summerhill committees, all contributed to a dynamic and varied social life. The principal difference between the pre- and post-war Summerhillians was the consciousness of and active involvement in politics. Robert thinks that Neill was rather wary of communists. "He was very disappointed that communism in Russia hadn't done what people hoped it would." Although it is true that Neill had strong left-wing sympathies at this time, and had made several favourable references to the 'brave experiment' of Communist Russia, he never allied himself to any political party. In 1937 he had spoken of Russia as a 'creative civilisation'. However, later that year his suspicions were aroused when his visa application was turned down by the Soviet authorities without explanation. Also, it was a matter of principle with him that, just as no child should be subjected to religious or moral propaganda, so it should be free from political moulding. He tolerated and accepted CP membership and activity amongst his staff, but did not approve of them involving the children. In fact Robert did help to send the *Daily Worker* round at one time. With the advance of fascism and Nazism, and the outbreak of the Spanish Civil War in 1936, it would have been impossible to keep politics out of Summerhill, especially as Spanish and German refugees began arriving at the school and several parents were actively involved in anti-right-wing organisations. "We all felt that Communism was the future in the 30s. We used to give up our supper on Saturdays to Spanish refugees. This was at the time of Guernica when a lot of people we knew joined the International Brigade."

The outbreak of war came as no surprise to Robert. "I remember sitting by Neill's radio when Chamberlain came on to announce that 'consequently this country is at war with Germany.' I can remember it very well. I'm also quite good on a lot of Churchill's wartime speeches, which I can remember." A few days after war was declared an extremely popular Austrian housefather, Tony [Antoine Oberleitner, aka Obert], was taken away by the police to be interned as an enemy alien. The Summerhillians were furious but there was nothing they could do. "Over 50 years later I met him again at a reunion party, the first time I'd seen him since I watched him being driven away in the back of a police car in 1939. After the war he'd emigrated to Canada."

The Mullers agree that the core of Summerhill was the weekly meeting. Although she did not participate much in the General Meetings herself – "I don't remember ever saying anything" – Biddy has no doubt of their value. "They were a good airing. People would volunteer to do things and problems did get sorted out. People always had more definite views if they were involved in committees, as Robert was."

Robert feels that the beneficial influences of the meetings have lasted into adult life. "I think I would have been totally impossible, even more horrible than I am, if I hadn't been to Summerhill, whereas I feel I have some good attributes now. I often chaired the meetings and found that a very useful experience. I think possibly they helped me understand other people's point of view, though I suspect Biddy might say I never understood anybody else's point of view. I feel that democracy worked well on the whole. Some groups would dominate for a time, but they came and went. If things didn't work, people would resent it and eventually remove them. That is the natural process of democracy. I'm a little bit cynical about democracy in the outside world. There's that wonderful passage in *1066 And All That* about the Magna Carta which says that 'everyone should be free (except the Common People)'. That just about sums up the Magna Carta."

"There was one very interesting term without democracy. One of the teachers, Cyril Eyre, had been confined to bed after a hockey injury. "I don't know how it came about but the General Meeting voted to make him dictator. We had a cracking term, though Cyril was probably worn out by it. From morning till night an unending succession of his deputies would bring him the community's problems and disputes to resolve and he adjudicated with the wisdom of Solomon. I think at one time Neill thought that Cyril might succeed him."

As Robert recalls, "Everyone was totally open about sex at Summerhill. We sometimes got smutty boys transferring from public schools. I remember one in particular, two or three years older than me – very much the smutty sixth-form type; very popular with the domestic staff, or so he liked to think; but he lost that within two or three terms. He became a thoroughly nice bloke. It was just the environment he'd been in previously. The general attitude towards sex of outsiders seemed pretty childish after Summerhill, and it still does."

Though the approach to sex and sex education at Summerhill has remained remarkably consistent over the years, perhaps the one major change has been in its attitude towards homosexuality. As Robert recalls: "There were the usual adolescent experiments in homosexuality, but these were short-lived and the general opinion was anti. Neill was definitely anti-homosexual. He thought it was an aberration, a sickness, probably a result of bad conditioning. I feel that myself. I'm not out to pillory them, but I'm inclined to feel it's not a natural thing. But I really don't know."

Robert and Biddy agree that there was real sex equality at Summerhill. "Girls had as much to say as anybody else on the committees. It depended on character, not male or female." The main difference being, in Robert's opinion, that "perhaps the girls were more realistic, less interested in theory."

After Summerhill

I left school with bags of self-confidence. Perhaps Summerhill people do seem a bit arrogant and feel they're a bit better than other people. One was aware of differences outside, certain things that didn't happen at Summerhill. People seemed more childish certainly. We used to say, 'Oh, well, it happened outside.' We thought we were a pretty superior lot, we Summerhillians. Even I find it somewhat annoying in others, and no doubt they do in me.

At the end of 1942/beginning of 1943 I had left Summerhill with the intention of joining the army as soon as I could. I did a year at the Guildhall, worked part-time in the family firm, and in my spare time formed Croydon Youth Drama and took an active part in the cadets where I ran the battalion magazine. I was soon promoted to under-officer; I think because I had a lot of self-confidence and people do accept you on your own evaluation to a large extent. I used to feel I could do things better. I was all of 17 when they put me in charge. I used to march my platoon to HQ whilst all the others were lying around smoking, waiting to be called on parade. I'd walk smartly up to the CO: 'Number Three Platoon ready for your inspection, sir!' He hardly knew what to do. We made the Home Guard look like Dad's Army. When we passed them I used to call out "Number Three Platoon, eyes right!" They were all over the place. All our 15- and 16-year-olds were much more efficient.

I joined the army proper in 1943/44, enlisting as a private, but contracted pneumonia and pleurisy together rather badly. A patch on the lung and various odd problems – so I couldn't go on active service and got invalided out after a year. But I enjoyed myself reorganising all the various departments that I got put in charge of. My status became much higher than my rank. However, when the time came I was glad to go. I didn't see myself as being in an army of occupation. I certainly wouldn't have been a professional soldier. I took it up keenly and got all the necessary certificates to become a qualified instructor, but once the war was as good as over I lost interest.

I'll never forget seeing the headlines: 'Americans drop bomb over Hiroshima. U235, the new uranium atom split,' and Mike Bernal phoning me up shortly afterwards and reminding me about the bedtime stories his father used to tell us some ten years previously. Sage [J.D.] Bernal had been working for several years on the theory of atomic energy. He used to tell us wonderful futuristic stories, which we thought of as rather like Jules Verne or H.G. Wells, about superbombs with tremendous destructive power, complete with references to U235. Though they'd seemed like science fiction stories at the time, they were really predictions. When Mike phoned me up it all came back to me. Unlike many people at that time I did not see the advent of the atom bomb as heralding a new age. There's always been something. I love castles, and I've spent a lot of time researching them, and I remember thinking that when black powder was first used to make holes in castle walls it must have been seen in exactly the same way. It must have been quite as momentous to their world at that time as the atom bomb was to ours. It would have changed their set-up one hundred per cent.

I was an enthusiastic supporter of the first post-war Labour government, but it was one of my very considerable annoyances at the time that I was old enough to die for my country but too young to vote. I thought the NHS was a magnificent achievement. I was very proud of it. Most Summerhillians were socialist at that time. Inevitably my experiences at Summerhill shaped me politically to some extent, but I don't think you'd find that every Summerhillian would call himself a socialist today. I feel it's become a very much misused term. We mustn't forget that Hitler was a national socialist, so I'm careful about using that word personally.

After demob I went back into the family business. Mother was keen for me to go to RADA because although she was very good at business she didn't venerate it and didn't want me to have anything to do with it. She would have liked a stage career herself. I could have gone fairly easily because there were plenty of scholarships around, but I never wanted to be a professional actor. I found learning lines drudgery. However, I've found my acting skills useful in business and lecturing. I enjoyed amateur acting and derived a great deal from my acting experiences at Summerhill, particularly Neill's spontaneous acting classes. He's quoted me several times in his books, though not by name.

I did find the business boring. It was failing. We were still making rackets by hand that would soon be made by machine. So it was a relief when after 10 years we sold out to Lillywhites. We got a very good price which Mother and I negotiated together. She had the necessary intuitive feelings and I did the front stuff.

Biddy and I met again in 1946/47. There hadn't been anything between us at Summerhill except I used to pull her pigtails sometimes in the breakfast queue. She'd left at 14.

Biddy recollects, "After the war I moved up to London and started working in one of the top ten dress houses as a seamstress. I enjoyed the work, particularly doing theatrical costumes when I joined Bermans the theatrical costumiers. A group of Old Summerhillians started meeting in Vicky's bar in the Shakespeare's Head in Carnaby Street. We preferred the company of other Summerhillians. We could talk to each other easily. It was like being part of a family. That was where Robert and I met again. We lived together for about a year before we got married. That was quite daring in those days. Our contemporaries were getting married. Some Summerhillians got married to each other, one or two married Summerhill teachers, others married outside. Some marriages lasted, some didn't. Ours has, even through working 24 hours a day in the pub. I don't think Summerhill made any difference as far as the success rate of marriages went. It was just typical of the times."

What I find funny in some marriages today is not that people get married and then get divorced. That's always happened. What does amaze me is why some of them bother to get married in the first place. Why don't they, since it's no problem, live together until they've finished with it?

In 1954, having sold up the business, I needed a job. I had been chairman of the board of directors of the Studio Club in Swallow Street, and after the manager left had taken over the running of it in my spare time, without pay. I was then asked to take the job on full-time as secretary-manager, which meant resigning from the committee. The Studio Club had been very successful in the past but had become slightly less so recently. I decided to build it up and the first thing I did was to close the membership. Everyone thought I'd gone totally raving mad, but in six months we had a queue of people waiting to join. I'd made it exclusive and therefore attractive. The next step was to improve the drinks sales. At that time liqueurs were an expensive classy drink, costing 1s 9d; I decided to put a range of liqueurs in optics – which was unheard of –and sell doubles for 2s 6d or 3s. Once again the committee said 'you're mad,' but it was a roaring success and the club made a lot of money. It's the Gulben-kian principle. The percentage goes right down but the overall sales and profit go up. The word got around and people started coming in droves. They were all falling about on liqueurs. Then I hit on the idea of selling cheap wine. I put a row of dirty little wooden barrels behind the bar, on tap, and I'd fill a plain bottle for five bob. I'd say, 'What do you want, plonk or super plonk?' That was also a tremendous success and pretty soon we were selling more wine in volume than most clubs sold in beer. We made a lot of money. It wasn't the easiest of jobs, we didn't finish till one o'clock in the morning, but it was very satisfying. Anybody who was anybody in the arts used to get into the Studio Club, a lot of whom are household names now, especially jazz musicians, because our house pianist, Alan Clare, was a brilliant player and they liked to drop in for a jam session. So we'd get all this wonderful music for free. John Dankworth and Cleo Laine were regulars, and Stephane Grappelli called in whenever he was over from Paris. He played for nothing once or twice. Len Deighton worked there part-time as a waiter while he was studying at the Royal Academy School of Art round the corner. Later he wanted to get a job on the Queens, going back and forth to New York, so I gave him a reference. Sometime after that he started publishing best-sellers. I was surprised when I picked up his book *Où est Le Garlic?* What little he knew about cooking he'd picked up at the club. But he had a good way of presenting it. Dylan Thomas came in a couple of times. There were also regular art exhibitions which would run for a month. A man came in one afternoon and sat there politely and quietly for quite a few minutes before I was able to attend to him. Eventually he chose five pieces and said, 'Would you please have them sent round by cab for me?' I was about to say, 'Stuff you, friend, I don't even know who you are or do I get any money or what,' when he showed me his card: Sir David Eccles, Minister of Education. I decided I could probably trust him to pay up.

There was music every night. It was always good fun going to work, though very hard. We had mad, gay, crazy nights. Could be a Valentine's night, whatever. Any excuse. I'd buy a lot of cheap lining paper to put up over the walls and get down anybody I could to decorate the place. Newspaper cartoonists like Raymond Jackson [Jak] and Lesley Grimes [Grimey]. These were the boys. In no time at all you had a wonderful décor. I made sure that at their hand, besides a brush, there was always a glass. The more they drank, the more uninhibited the design. That's all it cost us, wine, and a meal of course; I always made sure they were well looked after. It looked terrific.

I stayed nine years and tried very hard, within my own very obvious dictatorial limits, to run it as a democracy with the committee. I got on very well with the chairman. But you had to remember you had to run it, whatever the committee thought. You might get some silly ideas from one or two of them that wouldn't go. In 1963 I decided to leave. New people had come in at the top and the whole atmosphere changed. I was earning good money but I didn't like it any longer. I had been befriended by a very eminent caterer who taught me the business and I had studied, gone to night school and collected handfuls of odd catering certificates. I can write streams of letters after my name. This, together with my nine years' experience – we used to produce 150 to 200 meals a day in the club – left me well placed to apply for a manager's job with a brewery. I reckoned that by that time I could do everything except play the piano. Biddy and I applied as joint managers of a pub – 'Man and wife required' – and were successful.

Biddy adds: "I heard later they'd seen us coming across the road and said we looked like typical publicans, which rather annoyed me as I'd never worked behind a bar before."

We took on a pub with a Chinese restaurant upstairs. Most unusual then. The staff lived in and did the cooking but we were the managers. They put us on a large commission and a small salary, which is the way of English breweries, but we did very well. Fortune, in the shape of Egon Ronay, smiled on us. He gave us a good write-up which did us no end of good. It packed the place. We didn't even know he'd visited till the article appeared. By the second year our commission had outstripped our salary. I think they were very surprised.

After that we moved on to manage a function house with a staff of 30. Neither of us liked it terribly, but we made a lot of money for the brewery. It was the first time they'd made a profit at that pub in 15 years or something. Then they gave us the tenancy of the White

Hart at Puckeridge. I had another bit of good fortune. The writer Jack Trevor Story, whom I knew from the Studio Club, dropped in on his way back to London. We saw each other across the bar. We had a paralytic morning and the next day his column in the Guardian began, 'Met my old pal Bob Muller in the White Hart, Puckeridge... We had a lot of people come in on the strength of that.

For Biddy it was not quite the same: "I had mixed feelings about pub life. I enjoyed a lot of it a lot of the time and it was fun being a landlady, but it was also a big tie: we didn't have a holiday for years, and the kids didn't get much of a look-in. I was very much against going into pubs. I thought it was going to be absolutely rotten for the kids. I'd led a very insular life while Bob was working in the club and the children were small. I enjoyed being a landlady because I was meeting people. But I did neglect the kids rather from that point on. If you're running the pub successfully, you're giving up your life to it. I think the children feel that they were neglected and, in spite of both of us having gone to Summerhill, we didn't do a thoughtful enough job on their education. Being a parent is a commitment."

I held a different opinion. When I was at Summerhill I remember thinking the best thing adults could do was leave kids alone and let them get on with it. Even as a 17-year-old I thought it. My attitude to adults was, 'Piss off and let me get on with my life.' I was quite happy running it, thank you. That's how I felt and that's really what I've done. I now think differently. I now believe you should do parenting as a specific job, that is, bring up children. In which case I would probably opt out, because I haven't the ability, tact or patience to do it very well. My grandchildren are another matter. I can relate easily to them, just as a person, because I have no responsibility. I don't feel guilty because I don't think one can behave very differently from the way one's character is. Whatever one means to do one will be more or less oneself.

Biddy adds, "I think a feeling of having no restrictions, no rules, no regulations, doesn't really give a child a basis to work on. If you set down a few sensible house rules, not punishing rules, it gives them a stability."

I would agree with that. After all in Summerhill we didn't have total freedom, or as Neill was fond of pointing out, we didn't have licence.

The Mullers sent the children to school locally at first, then decided they should go to boarding school.

Biddy recalls, "Our daughter went to New Sherwood originally, which was meant to be a kind of mini-Summerhill, but this was not a success at all. It didn't have enough kids in it. A lot of them were weekly boarders and she got left there at weekends. It didn't work out. Then we sent them both to the Royal Russell Haberdashers' School, mainly because we knew the secretary and she recommended it. It was nearby in Surrey and a mixed school, though in practice the sexes were segregated. Neither of the children was particularly happy there. When we moved to the White Hart in Puckeridge we sent them both to Ware College in Hertfordshire, where our daughter won the Sebastian Earl award for design (top of the country in her year) and our son went on to make wonderful woodwork, furniture and buildings in Bristol, where he now lives. They each have a son and a daughter, so we have four grandchildren of whom we are extremely proud. So it turned out all right in the end."

After I'd been a tenant for five years I got fed up with the pub. I applied for a job as district manager and was appointed in January 1974. At the age of 48 I was by far the youngest of the district management team. I did this job for seven years and was responsible for 25 outlets from pubs to golf clubs. I acted as adviser to the tenants and did quite well. In 1980 I became a senior district manager and then in 1981 the Deputy General Manager, Retail. I was responsible for 125 outlets and over a thousand people. I enjoyed it, though less so in the last few years. In 1989 I was offered a good deal and retired. We then moved into our present home in Wenhaston, which was originally a couple of derelict farm-labourers' cottages in the middle of a field that we'd bought years before. In the holidays and at weekends we'd gradually done it up.

Since retiring we've been involved in local amateur dramatics and also gardening – we have a little over one acre to tend. In more recent years a lottery-funded arts centre has become established in nearby Halesworth and we very much enjoy attending their musical and dramatic presentations.

Unquestionably I gained a great deal from Summerhill. We had a lot of rules which enabled us to learn the difference between freedom and licence. All of life is a compromise, whatever you do and wherever you go. We weren't able to do whatever we wanted. Neill could be very firm and throw people out. He was never sloppy. There were stringent rules about what you did down town: there was no smoking, for example. But you did have power in your own sphere, though power was not conscious as such at Summerhill. You had a certain amount of power by serving on a committee, and later on as a junior cadet officer I had quite a lot of power. But with it came responsibility.

I think DIY is a very important part of a kid's upbringing and this was very much encouraged at Summerhill. I think I can turn my hand to just about anything. My attitude has always been 'buy a book and take a look' then have a go. I had a lot of good training at Summerhill. I always painted my own room, which was generally pretty grubby when I moved in, and made a good job of it. Every holiday when I came back, Mrs Lins would give me a different room. I cottoned on to what she was doing, which was to get all the rooms painted and decorated for nothing. After that I got a padlock and made sure my room was securely locked before I went home.

Choice over lessons is important, but guidance to stimulate interest is also useful. I think teachers should be consulted for advice about what to study. Also, it's not true that if you can't do a thing well it's not worth doing, which was Neill's attitude. I think he was wrong about that. You can still get a lot out of learning to play the piano even if you're not going to be brilliant.

The academic side of teaching in my day was exceptionally good, and the arts. Many pupils became high-fliers. Summerhill has always been an international school, which is probably an advantage. We had about 20 different nationalities. In those days the Scandinavians were best represented; nowadays it's the Japanese, I believe.

Biddy has a slightly different perspective: "My impression is that there were a lot of older hangers-on before the war, 18- and 19-year-old boys not doing much. Then of course they all went off to war. You don't get those older hangers-on nowadays."

A great deal of what Summerhill postulated in our day has come to pass. There is no longer corporal punishment, for example. It's impossible to say what people would have been like had they gone to other schools. Background and class do come into it. If you come from the middle class you are more likely to be successful, and before the war Summerhill was only possible for middle-class people. We are not all going to be equal and the successful people will succeed wherever they go. However, we could do much more to help the borderline ones, both for their own satisfaction and for their usefulness to society. So Summerhill still has relevance. Living out problems is still part of the therapy.

We have been back to Summerhill on various occasions, reunions and so forth, and inevitably find much has changed since our day. But the same happy and free atmosphere predominates under Zoë's leadership. Her achievement in keeping the school going is particularly praiseworthy in the face of government attempts to close it down. Summerhill clearly has a place to fill in the world of education as an example of what can be achieved by the methods of A.S. Neill.

Postcript (2011)

Robert and Biddy are living quietly in retirement in Suffolk. They enjoy wine tasting and Robert was for many years active in their local drama group. They have travelled to India on a number of occasions to visit The Banyan Tree, a charity in which a friend of theirs is very involved.

Hylda Sims
1942-47

Hylda Sims is unique amongst the people interviewed for this book in that her earliest years at Summerhill were spent in the beauty of Ffestiniog, Wales, where the pupils were evacuated during the war. The return to the post-war drabness of Leiston proved something of a disappointment – at least initially.

Hylda, who was strongly drawn to academic disciplines, was, she feels, liberated from a tendency towards priggishness which a traditional girls' grammar school education of the day would have developed in her. The roundedness of Summerhill education, which freed her socially and artistically, paved the way for a much more interesting and varied journey through life.

Hylda was born in 1932. Both her parents were married to other people when they ran off together. Her father, who was several years older than her mother, was a *crocus* – an itinerant trader selling patent medicines at markets. Itinerant traders in general were known as grafters. "I would describe his background as upper working class. He was a founder member of the Communist Party of Great Britain and before that a member of the Plebs League. He had a very strong anti-boss attitude." Her mother's background was skilled working class. "She was a tough and efficient manager." There is a family legend that Hylda's maternal grandfather invented stainless steel and received one pound for it. Hylda spent the first years of her life travelling around with her parents, staying at first in a variety of digs and later in a caravan that her father made. There were five elder half brothers and sisters who visited during the holidays.

At the outbreak of war in 1939 the family settled in Norwich where Hylda's mother started making fishcakes, which she supplied to hospitals, and also ran a café. "The business thrived and we began making money. By the end of the war my parents had acquired a very nice house on the Norfolk Broads, although my father, who was a romantic, always expressed a yearning to get back on the road."

Norwich came under heavy attack during the blitz and Hylda's parents decided to get her away to a place of safety. Many kids who might not otherwise have gone to Summerhill were sent there for this reason. Hylda remembers the air raids and going down into the shelter. "It was very scary, but like most children I felt myself to be immortal." Hylda's parents had read Neill's books about Summerhill and liked what they'd read. "At that time the Communist Party was far more radical in social terms than it later became and new educational ideas were very much on the agenda. Many of the pupils at Summerhill in those days were children of CP members, some of whom had fought in Spain in the International Brigade."

The Summerhill pupils had been evacuated to Ffestiniog in Wales, and the house at Leiston had been taken over by the army. Hylda's parents wrote to Neill asking if he would take her. Because of the war, the school was full up [both with children and adults, many of whom were refugees from Nazi Germany] and Neill replied that he didn't have any room. However, Hylda's father offered to lend Neill his caravan, which could sleep three children, and on those terms he accepted.

Hylda was happy to get away from her parents, from Norwich and from the schools she had gone to. "I'd been to a lot of schools on the road, staying sometimes for as little as a day, and disliked them all. At my primary school in Norwich I felt bored and antagonistic – and lost. I had the feeling of not knowing the ropes; not knowing what was expected of me. I thought Summerhill sounded a good place."

In the summer of 1942 Hylda and her parents travelled down to Ffestiniog with the caravan. "The weather was idyllic and that remote part of Wales was strikingly beautiful. The school was situated in an old mansion half-way up the side of a valley. It belonged to a Lord Newborough who rented it to Neill. There were sloping lawns and terraces, an empty swimming pool where meetings were held in fine weather, and a big tree with a rope for swinging. In the surrounding countryside were rocky woods where you could climb trees and a sheer hill behind that could be climbed up to the village.

There was a nearby lake in which you could go swimming. From the school windows you could see a mountain range of three peaks into which we would often go on expeditions. Sometimes we camped out there. There were no air raids to plague anyone."

Hylda remembers her first term well. "I was a bit of a know-all when I arrived and acquired the nickname 'The Walking Encyclopedia'. I was also physically modest and shocked and annoyed that the bathroom doors were without locks, so I came in for a good deal of ragging on both these counts, particularly from a boy named Michael Boulton whom I was half in love with because of his striking good looks. But by the end of term I'd begun to feel at ease and had made several friends."

Hylda found that the adults at Summerhill were very different from those she had previously encountered. "They spoke to you as one human being to another and always listened to the content of what you said. They didn't think what you ought to be doing was any different from what you were doing. So I felt released from unhealthy preoccupations with what adults were thinking and doing about me. I was able to absorb myself with intense enjoyment in the day-to-day living of my life."

A teacher Hylda remembers with particular fondness was Ulla, an Austrian refugee who taught sewing and dressmaking. "We loved going to her cosy room for our lessons. It had a European quality to it, rather like the photograph of Freud's study in Vienna." Being invited to staff's rooms was a very important part of Summerhill life.

There were some brilliant pupils there, Hylda recalls, many of whom went on to excel in adult life. "There was quite a strong intellectual climate. I myself was strongly attracted to academic work and went to most of the lessons." In addition to the high standard of teaching, there was the advantage of small classes, usually no more than five or six, and a relaxed informal atmosphere.

Although there were very good staff who stayed the course, there was also a lot of coming and going. A lot of people, Hylda feels, came for various reasons of their own which were perhaps not totally admirable. "I think there have been times all through Summerhill's life when adults came to Summerhill because it was a famous place where there was freedom, and they didn't really understand the implications of that freedom, didn't understand their responsibilities for the kids. The main thing that happens to them while they are at Summerhill is that they're searching out their own heads. That can be quite disastrous for the kids because they're not being properly looked after."

Some of the best teachers were quite formal in their teaching methods. Teaching at Summerhill has never been particularly experimental, quite rightly in Hylda's opinion. "I think there's too much emphasis on this in most schools." Neill called this experimentation 'sugaring the pill'. He strongly disagreed with the progressive educators whose concern was to make lessons more attractive and palatable. What was important to Neill was the absence of compulsion.

It was some time before Hylda noticed Neill. "I was surprised to learn that he was the old man I had often seen raking leaves at the side of the house." In those days Neill, under the influence of Freud and Stekel, was still giving PLs [private lessons – individual therapy sessions for kids who felt they needed them]. "I'd heard he asked things like, 'Do you envy your brother's penis?' or 'Do you think you are really a princess who was left on your parents' doorstep?' My friend Winnie had a PL every week and seemed to enjoy them. I felt a bit jealous but Winnie said you only had to ask, so I did." Hylda went to Neill's room one morning to find him sitting in his armchair. "He didn't say anything, just motioned me to sit down. I waited and nothing happened. After a while he lit his pipe, put the matches on the arm of his chair, picked up a newspaper, opened it out and disappeared behind it. I became increasingly impatient and peeved and said, 'Aren't you going to ask me some questions?' 'Nope.' So on impulse I grabbed the matches and set fire to the corner of his newspaper. Quite calmly he got up, put the newspaper on the floor and trod out the flames with his big boots. And all he said was, 'Good, I didn't think you had the guts to do that.' So that was my one and only PL."

Like many others Hylda remembers the integration and lack of gender stereotyping at Summerhill, but thinks that those feminists are wrong who claim that boys' and girls' interests and activities are only the result of social conditioning. "There was absolutely none of that pressure at Summerhill and yet differences emerged. That is not to say that there was no crossover. Most sports were shared events. I'm still a skilled table-tennis player, which surprises a lot of men. But boys and girls did tend to hang out in different gangs."

Although lessons were important it was the totality of life at Summerhill that Hylda recalls, the beauty of the surroundings, country walking, visits to the coast and to the cinema, music, drama and above all socialising and being on an easy footing with the opposite sex. "I think most of us were quite into having boyfriends and relationships and intrigues. I think of that as going on all the time while I was there. From every age. Flirting, changing partners, writing letters, joking and teasing and all those things were always important. I guess they are in any school, but at Summerhill it was more free."

It has already been noted that when Hylda first came to Summerhill she was, as she describes herself, physically modest, but that this soon went. "The first thing that journalists have always picked up on at Summerhill is the nudity, usually from a prurient point of view. But in fact you just feel that this is the carcass that you carry around with you. It's quite normal, everybody has one, so why all the fuss? Of course at the onset of puberty people became more conscious of themselves. Teenage boys are very often more self-conscious about that actually, about covering their genitals, than girls are." But there was no pressure either for or against swimming or sunbathing nude. "Some people would cover themselves sometimes, wear a swimming costume, and others wouldn't. But nobody made any comment about it. It was very down-to-earth."

In such a close-knit, some would say tribal, society was it possible to find space for oneself? In Hylda's opinion "it is probably much easier to get time on your own at Summerhill than anywhere else. The average child never has a moment's peace. It's very evident that in an ordinary school, which is frighteningly totalitarian, the aim is to account for a child's movements, and what they're making and doing with their time, every moment of their day. They never have a moment to themselves, except when they shut themselves in their bedroom at home. Even then, if they've got certain sorts – perhaps the average sort – of parent, the parent wants to know what they're up to, have they done their homework and so on. At Summerhill you don't have those kinds of pressures, so you can be on your own in your room or in the woods, or wherever, and no one will bother you."

But it was a very social life. Friendships were continued and developed during the holidays. "A huge aspect of Summerhill is just hanging out in somebody's bedroom, sitting around talking. There's an enormous part of that to it all. So that would be continued in the holidays."

Like everyone else, Hylda affirmed the central importance of the General Meeting. "I think I always went to the meetings, and I think this is true of the majority of kids. It probably took a while before I actually participated. You tend to sit there – and the little kids often don't participate – but then you get more used to it. You realise you really can express your opinions and they'll be listened to. Most kids started participating about the age of 10 or 11, which probably coincided with the beginning of their autonomy. It's very difficult for people to understand a GM if they haven't experienced it. Continuity and tradition play a big part. New kids become part of an established culture which, though it may undergo minor revisions, remains in essence the same. It's infinitely better organised than parliamentary debates which on the one hand are incredibly formal, but on the other there's all that barracking that goes on. You don't get that at Summerhill at all. Unruly elements are dealt with by on-the-spot fines, or in extreme cases people may be ordered to leave. So it's quite a strict thing in many ways."

Hylda draws a distinction between the problem kids and the period of unruly behaviour which many ordinary kids go through. "Neill always claimed there was this gangster period – and I think there could be some useful statistical work done on the sort of ages when that takes place. And I'll bet you anything it is, particularly for boys, when they are coming to puberty and are really interested in developing their autonomy. And therefore the average school, which is telling them what to do and expecting them to sit and attend to their lessons, is just not at all suitable for them. This is the point at which they break out. But really one should work out that that's a pretty natural thing to do at that age and think of other things to offer them."

Problem kids as such were a minority. "The community knew which of them were just arsing about and needed to be fined or told to stop, and the people who, it was recognised, actually needed a bit of tolerance and leeway. The meeting was very good about that. Most kids who started off being quite difficult straightened themselves out over the course of years."

The success of the community, Hylda feels, is very much dependent upon having a group of strong 14- to 16-year-olds. "We had a very good group while I was there, some of whom were extremely bright; good at debate and responsible in carrying out their duties." Does Summerhill function better with brighter kids? "I don't know whether you could say that the more intelligent people had a greater awareness of social responsibility. I think it's dangerous to generalise about that. I would suspect that those people had quite a rich intellectual life at home; it wasn't just a genetic thing. Certainly on the whole I would think your more delinquent kids would not come from such bright backgrounds, but it's very hard to say."

Another significant feature of Summerhill is the absence of intellectual divisiveness or kudos attached to academic success. "If you work in a state school or a private school, which I have, you are aware that this division is very apparent. There was this jargon in comprehensive school that you were either a bod or a boffin. If you're a bod you absolutely shun lessons whenever you can, and reject the establishment, and go round being a bit of a tearaway. If you're a boffin you hang about and listen to your teacher, do your homework promptly and generally suck up a bit, and that's what you're like. And the bods and the boffins mutually despise each other. Well, you just don't get that happening at Summerhill. People who were clever at lessons would have no problem relating socially to people who weren't so clever. Everybody would know that those people were clever, but they didn't think that they were therefore superior individuals." Perhaps this is partly due to the fact that everyone had a feeling of equality before the Summerhill laws. There was also much more interaction between the different age groups than is customary in large schools. "One would feel at ease in the company of adults or bigger kids. I think when you're a younger kid you like to be with older kids: you're learning from them – a bit of an acolyte. I think that's a natural thing. One of the unfortunate aspects of the wider educational system is that there isn't that opportunity for a mixing of ages, and the older kids don't have this caring role. Summerhill is more like a large extended family. But there aren't the feuds and jealousies that often occur in real families, and because you don't have the same parents, you don't have the emotional difficulties that that can cause."

Cultural inclusiveness was another important feature of Summerhill life. Nothing was considered in or out, too highbrow or too lowbrow. "There was a participatory approach to life in general, a feeling not of reverence but of wanting to join in. Nothing felt like too much. You felt you could do things without knowing all the scientific principles. There was for example a very free approach to the study of literature. You were encouraged to have and express your own opinion."

Hylda's voracious reading encompassed *Anne of Green Gables*, Richmal Crompton's 'William' stories, Dickens and Yeats. As well as his spontaneous acting classes, Neill held weekly play readings where, from about the age of 12, Hylda came to appreciate Ibsen. Self-written plays co-existed with productions of Shakespeare. There was a school jazz band and a choir [in which Hylda sang] organised by another refugee, Erna Gal, specialising in European folk songs. A good collection of records by top-quality jazz musicians such as Louis Armstrong, Duke Ellington and Nellie Lutcher were played at the Saturday night dances.

Hylda remembers the last years at Summerhill as being dominated by love affairs and taking part more in committees and plays. "I think the girls were more mature and prominent in organisation." Boarding schools for or against? Hylda has no doubt that being away from home was a definite advantage. "It allowed one to blossom and grow as an individual."

After Summerhill

I left Summerhill when I was 15 to go to ballet school in London. I stayed for a couple of years, and though I enjoyed it I realised I was not that good and was not prepared to put my life into it, so I went on to Battersea Poly – where there were a lot of other Summerhillians – to take my matriculation. A favourite Saturday night haunt was the Studio Club in Piccadilly which was run by Robert Muller. We gradually began to expand the group to include other young people, though there was a conscious feeling of them and us. We found many of them childish and repressed with strange sets of values. Those who fitted in well were described as 'quite Summerhillian'.

After I matriculated I did various jobs, including working in a late-night bookshop in Oxford Street, and began my first serious love affair. When I was 20 I went to teacher training college. It was partly to escape from this affair, and partly the attraction of qualifying to earn a living wage. I met Ivor Cutler, who was teaching at Summerhill in the early fifties, and he taught me to play guitar and I became involved in the folk revival. I played in coffee houses, doing Josh White covers, that sort of thing, and I also joined a youth choir. I qualified as a primary teacher, but only worked now and again when I needed some money. Then I met my husband Russell Quay, who was a painter of jazz musicians and a musician himself. When skiffle began we founded The City Ramblers. We used to play in London streets and later on we went off touring Europe in a bus, busking and clubbing. When we came back in 1957 we discovered that skiffle was in the hit parade. Around this time I also became pregnant with my first daughter, Viv.

We got a recording contract and a tour. I was the lead singer. We appeared on *6.5 Special* – one of the first TV pop programmes – and regularly on BBC Radio's *Skiffle Club* and opened The Skiffle Cellar in Greek Street, Soho. This lasted a couple of years. Then Russell went bankrupt and lost the club. Everything collapsed. Russell was very careless with money. It was an horrendous time. The marriage finished and I got offered a job as a minstrel singing old English songs in an Elizabethan restaurant where I continued to work, on and off, for the next 19 years.

In 1964 I went on a tour on behalf of that company to commemorate the 4th centenary of Shakespeare's birth – initially to Canada and then the States. I happened to be playing at Plaza 9, the club in the New York Plaza Hotel, at the same time the Beatles were staying there for their first American tour. Beatlemania was huge and because I was English I kept being mobbed by Americans who assumed I must be one of their party. I made TV appearances right across Canada and went to Italy, and when I came back I played the Troubadour Coffee Bar in London. I was making enough money to send both of my daughters to Summerhill.

In 1967 I entered university to read Russian Studies. I graduated with a 2.1. Then I went to the LSE and did a further three years' postgraduate studies. I enjoyed university life. I've always enjoyed learning, and unlike the other students I had no hesitation about plunging in and writing an essay expressing my own opinions, without reference to books of criticism. This was definitely a legacy of Summerhill. The other students were very hesitant about putting forward their own ideas. But by the end of the course we had moved to the middle ground – they were gaining in confidence and I was referring to books more.

In 1973 I started the Lifespan community with Freer Spreckley, taking my younger daughter with me. She didn't really enjoy Summerhill. In fact neither of my daughters enjoyed it as much as I had. There were a number of reasons for this. It was partly because my own life was unsettling for the children, but also I think they went away to school too young. I would not now send children away to school until the age of 11 or 12. They need their parents up to that age. Summerhill was at a fairly low ebb in the sixties. Neill was very old and the quality of teaching was not good. There was also insufficient nurture and care for the very young children.

I stayed at Lifespan for two years. I found it inspiring but hard and bitterly cold. I met my new partner there and in 1975 returned with him to London. I needed a job in order to get a mortgage so I went back into teaching; for the first time on a regular basis. I taught in Peckham Manor Boys' School from 1976 to 77. This was horrendous. Nasty, brutish and long. Then thankfully I was head-hunted by Kingsdale, a mixed school, much more civilised, where I taught English part-time. After that I did a TEFL course and was offered a job in Spain. I went there for a year and had a brilliant time. On my return I worked for a Business English school. When they moved to Salisbury I started my own English school on an Enterprise Allowance, also specialising in business students. I ran it on a part-time basis for about ten years.

In 1990 my relationship ended. We divided the profit from the sale of our house, but though I was able to make a substantial down payment on my current house, I needed to earn more money to pay the increased mortgage, so I went back into state education. But this time working at an Individual Tuition Centre in Peckham for kids who weren't coping at ordinary school. The Summerhill approach worked perfectly here and I got a permanent post working three days a week, continuing to work part-time at my language school and writing in my spare time. This was a very positive experience, but after London's ILEA was abolished individual tuition came under threat and has now been phased out completely. I now get on with my writing which has become the great absorbing interest in my life. I've written three novels, one of which, *Inspecting the Island*, based on the Summerhill idea (a kind of riposte to *Lord of the Flies*), has been published by a small press – Seven-Ply Yarns. I also write poetry and songs – my recent collection is *Sayling the Babel*, published by Hearing Eye – and until recently ran *Poetry and Jazz* in Covent Garden (at the Poetry Café) on Saturday nights. This has now been replaced by *Fourth Friday.*

Over the years I've found that things have not improved in state schools. Every time I went back with one of my pupils from Individual Tuition – who are expected to reintegrate with mainstream schools – I hoped to see that things had got better. But they never had. In fact I suspect they're getting worse. I feel there's not much hope for it. When you see what's going on in education, and you see the way people are batting on about things, you think, 'Christ, it's 2004, for God's sake. People are still talking about 1904.' If comprehensive schools were broken down into smaller units and democracy introduced, and there was the will to make it work, it could be done. In fact I think such places could be as good as or better than Summerhill.

Kids who go to Summerhill sometimes have parents who are screwed-up or screwy about certain things. So that's a limitation. Whereas I think the kind of kids you would meet in an ordinary school, or at least the unit where I worked, were often very promising 'ordinary' kids, and given a modicum of reasonable treatment they would be excellent kids and adults. What never fails to amaze me is how the kids at the IT Centre, who were mostly reckoned to have really bad backgrounds and a history of being trouble to everybody – how incredibly sensible they became when people were quite nice to them. For some kids schools are just like torment, every day of their lives. If you remove that torment a great many of them are quite all right.

Other schools could learn much from Summerhill. It would be great if state schools could get even some of the way there. After all it is the genuine relationship of adults and kids that is most important. There's a certain sincerity in the behaviour of Summerhillians. Neill used the word sincerity and I think that's absolutely evident, both at Summerhill and in other schools which are progressive; that the kids are not putting on an act. Whereas it seems to me that at the average school the kids have to put on an act for adults, either behaving atrociously or as if butter wouldn't melt in their mouths; which comes across as a bit of a drag really.

I would say you were brainwashed at Summerhill, but it was a benevolent form of brainwashing which included free choice. There are some aspects of Neill's attitude which were perhaps naive or simplistic. Summerhill often could have had and should have had better teachers, but perhaps, at certain periods in its history, because of certain ways it's been organised, or the fact it's an isolated community, or lack of money, that's something it hasn't been able to do very much about.

I don't think anyone has done it better than Neill. I don't think anyone has attempted anything quite so radical and brave and at the same time so practical and sensible. The basic fundamental principles of Summerhill – the principle of the meeting and freedom to stay away from lessons, and the principle of equality between adults and kids and the importance of being able to play and do what you want to do as long as it doesn't impinge on the freedom of others, all those ideas seem to me just fundamentally sensible.

Summerhill couldn't do everything, but some kids from difficult backgrounds were saved by going there. I myself feel saved. I might well have become insufferable and even more opinionated had I gone to a traditional girls' school. I can envisage myself as having become a priggish headmistress. But Summerhill encouraged a sense of fun and spontaneity. Above all, Summerhill has given me a fundamental sense of well-being which has lasted throughout my life.

Postscript (2011)

In 2008 I co-edited *Waterwords* – poems written beside Brockwell Lido in South London; published by BLU. In 2009, Hearing Eye published my collection, *Reaching Peckham*, a story in 40 poems. This was also issued as a CD with original music, including compositions and performances by two Old Summerhillians, Warabe Tatekoji and Lucien Crofts, and a former Summerhill teacher, Sarah Barton.

I continue to co-run the monthly *Fourth Friday* – poetry and acoustic music – at the Poetry Café and do the occasional gig as part of The City Ramblers Revival. I have also written a number of novels, one of which *Inspecting the Island* (Seven-Ply Yarns, 2000), is based is based on Summerhill.

Léonard Lassalle
1950-54

It is interesting to note the degree to which children who were at Summerhill during Neill's tenure remember him. Unlike many originators, Neill refrained from imposing his presence or views. Indeed, it was against his nature. Those who claimed that Summerhill 'was' Neill, and predicted that it would die with him, were quite wrong. Some former pupils scarcely remember him, except as a comforting background figure. For Léonard Lassalle, however, Neill was a pivotal influence who liberated him psychologically from a fraught childhood.

Léonard Lassalle was born in Nice, France, in 1937 and spent his earliest years under the German occupation. Although the valley in which he lived was not garrisoned, there were resistance fighters in the mountains and violence all around him.

Life at home was not without strife. "Though I had a very loving and liberal mother, my relationship with my stepfather was not good." Léonard never had the chance to meet his real father, a Jewish artist, a painter from Paris. His early education after the war's end was unusual but not ideal. "The school was run by a couple of Marxist lesbians. Although progressive they were quite strict, and set in their communist ideas."

Léonard's mother heard of Neill's school before the war and brought Léonard and his sister over to England, even though she had very little money. The full fees could not be met but the children were accepted and an arrangement made. This was typical of Neill, who rarely let money stand in the way of a child's attending Summerhill if he felt the child would benefit and the parents were behind it.

Léonard arrived not able to speak a word of English, though he quickly picked it up. He found Summerhill very scruffy and terribly cold in the winter – "especially for a young boy like me coming from the South of France. In the Carriages, where I slept, it was not unusual to wake up with ice on the sheets." Heating often made it worse.

"I remember getting a paraffin heater into my room and waking up with my sheets wringing wet. At first I suffered terrible rheumatism, but after about six months I adjusted to the weather."

However, the adjustments to the weather and the language were trifling compared with the inner changes Léonard was to undergo. "I was quite aggressive when I first came, because I think I felt insecure, not having a father." In fact Léonard was responsible for the only act of actual violence he encountered at Summerhill. "An older boy, an American named Jimmy who came from a difficult home background, used to tease me about my inability to speak English. One day I'd had enough. Something exploded inside me and I chased Jimmy, got him on the ground and began raining punches down on him." Suddenly something made Léonard stop and look up. "A ring of children had formed around us. They were all looking on with amazed – not disapproving – expressions on their faces. I immediately felt uncomfortable and ashamed. 'What are you looking at?' One of them replied in an astonished voice: 'We have never seen anything like this at Summerhill before.' Immediately all the hate and hostility for Jimmy went out of me and I got to my feet. Nobody cold-shouldered me and life went on as if nothing had happened. Jimmy and I became good friends." This was the Summerhill way of dealing with anti-social behaviour. "There was always a separation made between the act and the person." During the course of my interviews, I came across numerous instances of this approach of approving the child whilst disapproving his action. In Léonard's opinion it is not a wishy-washy idealism, but a robust, pragmatic approach that invariably produces the desired result of socialising the individual.

Another incident had an even more profound effect on Léonard. In fact, it was life transforming. "I'd come to Summerhill with an inner compulsion to paint. From the beginning I spent long hours in the art room, putting my lugubrious feelings on paper, working entirely from my subconscious. I didn't realise how unhappy I was most of the time." Although during the day Léonard would be cheerful and feel very happy, every night he would cry himself to sleep. Nobody else knew about this; it all came out in his pictures. Many of them were macabre. One he remembers depicted a hand being severed by a bloody axe; another, a convict behind bars looking cruel or lost.

It was through his painting that Léonard had his first direct encounter with Neill. "One day Neill called me to his office. It was the first time he'd really spoken to me alone.

'You seem like a cheerful sort of boy.'

'Oh, yes, Neill, I am.'

'Are you happy here?'

'Yes, very.'

'But you cry at night, don't you?'"

Léonard was astonished that anyone should have discovered his well-kept secret.

'How do you know that?'

'I've seen your paintings.'"

Léonard was shaken to the core. "I immediately burst into tears and a great flood of gratitude and warmth welled up inside me. It was as if Neill had entered into the deepest part of me and understood me. From that moment on I felt him as a secure presence. I loved him like the father I'd lost and never known. And I never again cried at night."

Although most of the Summerhillians who knew Neill feel a tremendous warmth and respect for him, Léonard, who perhaps untypically has a regard for the spiritual and mystical in life, was moved to express his feelings for Neill in quasi-religious terminology. "In my eyes Neill was a saint. He had an astonishing gift for being able to understand, enter into and love other people. It was as if he had been brushed by the wing of an angel. He had purified himself. There was no self-interest left in him, only love for others."

But Summerhill was not dependent on Neill alone. Léonard spoke in glowing terms of the vitality, the happiness and interest of everyday life. So many factors contributed to its wholesome influence: the teachers who had the gift of making their subjects come alive and with whom one could relate in a relaxed and friendly manner on a basis of human equality, where age difference and arbitrary authority played no role [among these was Ivor Cutler, later to become a well-known writer and entertainer]; the critical importance of the General Meetings – perhaps one of the few genuinely democratic assemblies ever to have been created; the complete absence of sex-repression which, far from leading to promiscuity, resulted in natural temperance and discrimination – what the psychoanalyst and lifelong friend of Neill, Wilhelm Reich, called "sex economy". There was an enormous amount of physical affection. "Before going to bed we, the older boys, would kiss all the girls goodnight. Some girls – usually the most attractive – one would linger over; with others it would be a perfunctory affair, but no girl was ever left out of this nightly ritual." On the other hand, Léonard has the impression that the girls sometimes regarded the boys as being rather childish – "though they were always fond of us and sympathetic. But sometimes they would gang up and order the boys out of the room. They were far more mature."

Children enjoyed life at Summerhill so much they often did not want to go home for the holidays, Léonard recalled. "I remember a boy called Philip hanging on to a seat at the railway station and screaming that he didn't want to leave. He grew up into a very nice guy."

After Summerhill

I left Summerhill at 15 because I wanted to get back to France and take the Baccalaureate, rather than sit for the General Certificate. I enrolled at a lycée in Cannes – Troisième – but quickly discovered I wasn't a scholar. I also found the atmosphere appalling – stupid and aggressive. There was a great deal of cruelty and anti-social behaviour. To me the teenagers there appeared somehow immature. Everything they were going through I had got out of my system years before. I couldn't make a connection with them and after three months I left.

I dropped all plans of taking the *bac* and decided instead to devote myself to painting. I attended an art school in Paris for the next two years. Even here I found most of the adults childish and disinclined to work. But I wanted to work. Why else go there? I had bags of self-motivation, the legacy of Summerhill, working within me. I devoted most of my time to life drawing and designing posters. In fact I soon was able to support myself with my poster designs.

I was astonished that people at the school, much older than me, lacked any self-motivation and seemed afraid of intelligent conversation about one's feelings. Most of these people's conversations were trivial and shallow. On the other hand they could be amusing and one laughed a lot. Also my teacher was excellent.

At 18 I returned to England and enrolled with the Central School of Arts and Crafts in London. This was partly because it was cheaper in England – my money would last longer. After the first year my financial situation improved as I won a scholarship. Also, I further increased my income by doing advertising. I remember having one poster everywhere on the London underground. I got plenty of freelance work in advertising and became rather successful. I designed covers for magazines, including *Ambassador*.

Then I began to feel terrible about persuading or manipulating people through advertising and decided to stop. Although my posters involved fine art work they were, I felt, increasingly corrupting my paintings. From that moment on I devoted myself to fine art only.

At this time I met my future wife, Melinda, and we decided to go to France where I would paint. I exhibited and sold my work in Nice, but then I found I was required to paint in a particular style, and orders started to arrive. I didn't want to do this, so I decided once again not to pollute my real work and began decorating pots to make money whilst I went on painting how I wanted to paint, developing my own style. Also Melinda and I began making scarves – batiks and dyed silk – to sell to shops. This was good fun and made us a living. In 1959 we were married.

In 1960, when I was 23, I felt I was becoming lazy and uncreative. It was time for a change. I had an accident and the money I received in compensation for this paid for a trip to Paris. By this time Melinda was pregnant.

In 1957 I'd received my first call-up papers. This was the time of the Algerian war, which I was determined to avoid. I fasted for two weeks before my medical and was declared unfit for service. I'm naturally skinny and the shedding of another half-stone made me look like someone suffering from prolonged malnutrition. The next year I was called up again. Once again I fasted and was absolved for another year. Once I was installed in Paris I began designing a shop interior, but in 1960 I received my third and final call-up papers. This time, to make doubly sure, in addition to fasting I took a sauna shortly before my medical and this time I was let off military service for ever. Complete exemption.

We stayed five years in Paris, until 1965. I was hard-up for a great deal of the time and found it necessary to do all sorts of odd jobs, including simultaneous translating for international conferences. I was able to support my wife and child on this, though we were still poor. We were living over a stable which I converted into a living comfortable space. Then by accident I got involved in the antiques trade and found I had a natural skill at selling. By 1965 we had three children and I was making a reasonable living. Perhaps it was my real father's Jewish blood that helped me with my marketing skills. Then we decided to educate our children in England.

We went firstly to London, where we were unable to find any-where permanent to live, then to Bridport where another child was born. We moved into a croft in Wales and continued to be poor, but in my quest for antiques I discovered a wooden angel which I sold for enough money to enable us to move to Tunbridge Wells where we later bought a house which I got for a low price (with money borrowed from the bank). I also opened an antiques shop in the Pantiles. Then my grandmother died and there was enough in her bequest to buy the lease for the shop, whilst the other small part of the inheritance enabled me to buy stock for the shop.

In 1967 our fifth child was born, and we eventually went on to have seven. One of my sons later worked with me in the antiques business and I was able to devote myself to interior design work for various well-heeled people including cabinet ministers and rock stars. Subsequently I returned to France where I work as a fresco painter and designer.

I was quick-tempered as a young man, with an authoritarian hereditary trait that, in spite of my mother's and Neill's influence, I was not entirely successful in overcoming. When it came to being with the children, I was not always able to be an example of patience, and struggled with my heredity. As time went on I improved. By the time we'd had our seventh child I was just beginning to turn into the sort of parent I wanted to be. I had never been physically violent, but sometimes took the little trouble-maker child out of the room. Summerhill taught me to be myself. I found it unpleasant to feel anger and suffered for my impatience; I found my wife and my own mother, who had not been to Summerhill, had more patience than I had.

Melinda had more intuitive understanding of the Summerhill method of raising children. Perhaps I taught her the theory and introduced her to the method, but with her peaceful nature she was able to put it into practice.

Other parents and friends were critical about the way we raised our children. They thought us too free. We never made them tidy up, or behave politely, or punished them for social offences. We had no prohibitions against swearing and certainly never taught them good manners. Those same people now find our children charming and well-balanced. At home they were often difficult and self-centred, but outside with their friends always caring and loving. They suffered from authority at school, but never rebelled. Sometimes they could be arrogant with teachers. They stood up for themselves and others. Often they kept quiet about their problems at school. It was as if they wanted to protect us, their parents. Schools can be very stupid. I found that I had had a better education at Summerhill, even in the formal sense, than my children received at their state comprehensive.

We made a point of never asking our children to do anything.

We never asked them to do their homework from school, but they often did. We never asked them to clear up their own mess, but they often did clear up their own mess. They are perhaps too soft-hearted and caring. At least one of my children had a reaction against this. He superficially hardened himself in order to protect his own being. "You have left me too open," he once accused me. But they are all very different. Of course they have all stood up to their father at times, and to each other at different stages during puberty. This is natural. They aren't angels. But it's the sort of person you turn into, not what you were, that is important. The child is father to the man. Today all my children are completely self-assured, independent and getting on with their lives.

I made a point of being back home after work by six every night so I could spend the evening with my family. We had lots of parties and walks and a rich social life. Of course there were sometimes difficulties and arguments. All children are different. Not everything is clear and perfect. My children had to accept too that I wasn't perfect.

We didn't have a TV in the house when the children were younger. We thought it too strong a drug for young children to resist. There was never a TV in Summerhill in Neill's day. Now they have one. I can't think it's healthy. TV invades the imagination of young children. All my children were inventive and made up their own games.

I couldn't have afforded to send my own children to Summerhill. But that isn't the only reason. I wanted to enjoy my children as they grew up around me. If there had been a day school like Summerhill I would certainly have sent them there. Free boarding schools may be necessary for kids whose parents live abroad, or kids who come from unsatisfactory homes but, generally, if the parents are free in their approach, the effects of ordinary repressive schools will not be too destructive. My message to parents is trust your kids. Back them up even if they do something wrong. Don't criticise or disapprove of them. Nothing and no one is perfect, but you must have faith that in the end things will turn out for the best.

Postscript (2011)

I now live in Provence with my wife Melinda. We have to date 16 grandchildren. All our seven children have children themselves. They seem to cope well with their lives, although this does not mean that they do not experience suffering.

Melinda is a potter and I paint, something I stopped doing while raising our children. Painting has always been, for me, a true reflection of my talent; I feel in harmony with myself when I paint. Isn't the most important thing in life to feel at home in your being?

My ideas have not changed much in recent years, but I feel that I have. I am now not so radical; softer and understand more deeply my own nature. I am more patient with myself as with others. My mother's love, Neill's love, my wife and my children's love, all this love is no doubt responsible for my happiness today.

As a consequence of an accident I had, since 1995 my vision deteriorated so much that after 2007 I could not continue to paint and turned to writing. I have been working on my autobiography. Since the age of 19 I have been active in a spiritual movement called Subud.

Brian Anscombe*

Robert Townshend

Elizabeth Pascall as a child

Elizabeth Pascall

Mike Bernal

Robert Muller

This picture, which is assumed to be Brian Anscombe, is extracted from a group photo taken in 1925 when Brian was at the school. There are 10 pupils and three staff in it – the exact number of people at Summerhill at the time, according to Brian's recollection.

Hylda Sims as a child

Hylda Sims

Léonard Lassalle as a child

Léonard Lassalle

Freer Spreckley

Ethan Ames

Danë Goodsman

Lucien Crofts

Clare Harvie

Warabe Tatejoke

Rhoda Goodall as a child

Rhoda Goodall

Abigail Taylor as a child

Abigail Taylor

A.S. Neill, founder of Summerhill

Freer Spreckley
1955-63

*The feature of Summerhill that most often inflames passions is the
complete lack of coercion – or even encouragement – over attendance at
lessons, with the perfectly understandable concern that turning out an
illiterate or innumerate person would be an enormous handicap to them
in later life. The story of Freer Spreckley is a most enlightening example
of this educational philosophy in action. A self-confessed 'problem kid',
he left Summerhill unable to read or write and yet went on to lead what
to many people would seem an enviably rich and worthwhile life.*

*When I first met Freer he was in his early forties, a strongly-built
handsome man with grey hair, comparatively recently married to Sally,
a former Summerhill teacher whom he had met on one of his visits to the
school. They lived with their first child in a quiet suburb of Nottingham.
The home was filled with the many artefacts that Freer has collected in
his travels, and the books, mostly non-fiction, that he has devoured since
teaching himself to read in his early twenties.*

*It was difficult to reconcile this affable, thoroughly well-integrated
man with the wild, sometimes nightmarish kid that he and others who
were there at Summerhill at the same time remember him to have been.
It is not surprising now to learn that he is descended on his father's
side from an 'upper middle-class lineage', but as one contemporary at
Summerhill told me: "When I first met Freer I would have thought he
came from the thickest, most ignorant type of background imaginable."
Freer is perhaps the most triumphant vindication of Neill's philosophy
of the healing power of freedom and approval that one could imagine.
Significantly, I have met other Old Summerhillians – remarkably sane
and down-to earth people – who told me they would probably have ended
up in prison or psychiatric hospitals had it not been for Summerhill.*

Freer Spreckley's mother was a working-class girl from the East End
of London who died when he was two. His father, David Spreckley,
came from a wealthy family with a strong military tradition – at

least ten consecutive generations of officers. This name, Freer, denotes the family's Scandinavian origins rather than, as one might imagine, having been conferred on him as a symbol of his father's aspirations. Traditionally it had always been a middle name in the Spreckley family, but Freer's father broke with tradition in this, as in so many other things. Maybe it did have something to do with Spreckley Senior's middle-class revolt after all. He was commissioned at Sandhurst, but shortly before the Second World War resigned his commission and became a conscientious objector. His family immediately disinherited him.

During the war David Spreckley lived in a commune which, among other things, developed the concept of wholefoods in this country. After the war he worked for a while as an actor in the West End, then some time after his wife's death he left London to set up a mobile bookshop, selling books on organic farming. Freer spent the next three years with his father travelling all over England to agricultural shows and colleges, occasionally attending schools. "I didn't get on with the other kids or the school environment, and my father never put any pressure on me to go. I couldn't read or write, which I think contributed to my feeling of isolation."

When Freer was six or seven, his father's new female partner came to live with them. "I strongly resented this, so it was then my father decided to send me to Summerhill – something he'd always intended doing." Although David Spreckley didn't have very much money of his own he was able to persuade the local council to pay the fees. Freer was horrified at the prospect of being sent away. "I can't remember much about that period, but having subsequently read Wilhelm Reich's theories of character armouring, I think I was simply protecting myself against pain by shutting out the experience."

However, he has vivid recollections of his first day at Summerhill. "My father went off with Neill to make arrangements, and I was left to wander around in a state of confusion. Then some kids invited me to play football with them in the lounge and from that moment on I felt comfortable. In fact, far from feeling homesick, when I went home in the holidays I felt schoolsick."

Although Freer had been raised as a vegan – his father being one of the earliest vegans in this country – at school he began eating meat. "The Summerhill diet was excellent," Freer recalls. "Fresh meat and vegetables, brown bread and plenty of milk." In this respect also, Freer feels, Summerhill was a pioneer. "At that time it was very rare to see brown bread in an ordinary baker's."

For the first time in his life Freer met other kids from lone parent backgrounds. "In the 1950s this was very rare. The attitude of society was that single-parenting was wrong. My father had had disapproval expressed to him about this. But at Summerhill it felt normal." The children compared one another's families and talked freely about them. "Some said they didn't like or even hated their parents. The parents seldom visited. This was probably not true of the majority of kids there, but the problem kids tended to hang out together."

Freer's gang were all problem kids from broken homes, mostly from fairly well-off middle-class backgrounds. "I think that many of the parents, though approving of Summerhill, would probably not have sent their children there if the homes had stayed together."

Although he was uninterested in academic subjects, Freer liked and attended all the practical lessons such as knitting and sewing (not considered at all girlish at Summerhill), pottery, brass-beating (with Neill) and woodwork. "And I was always repairing bikes." Neill's stepson, Peter Wood – a very good potter who had studied under Bernard Leach – got the pottery going and Freer, although he makes no claims himself, is remembered as the outstanding potter of his generation.

The art teacher, Harry Hering, gave him a lot of encouragement with painting and drawing. "All of these people were good teachers, principally because they were good at what they were doing themselves. Kids watched them and wanted to learn their skills." In other words, many of the teachers were first and foremost enthusiasts who would practise their skills regardless of whether or not the pupils joined in. So education was caught rather than taught. Arguably the same principle could be said to apply to the morality of Summerhill.

There were no lessons on religion or ethics, but morality was transmitted through the experience of real-life issues.

Apart from brass-beating, Freer spent a short time in Neill's maths group where the emphasis was on mental arithmetic presented in the form of a story containing lots of numbers in it and finishing with a calculation. It would probably be labelled a Special Needs class nowadays, Freer feels. "I found the stories very entertaining and became adept at coming up with the right answer." This was probably his only contact with academic education.

Freer remembers that all the kids liked Neill. "He was just there, always unobtrusive. You didn't see him that often and he never invaded the kids' environment, but he was a strong, likeable presence." Freer's main contact with Neill was through his Private Lessons. "I had a lot of those. Helping you to articulate your feelings was an important part of the process. He would talk about a parent disappearing – whether divorced or, in my case, dead – and ask what you felt about it. Most parents in those days would not discuss these matters with their children; my own father had never done so. Perhaps today there is more openness about this." Nowadays, at Summerhill, this articulation of feelings about parental loss tends to happen with members of staff, but then it was specifically Neill's province. "These chats were a subtle business. You hardly noticed them in a way, because they took up such little time, and you never discussed them with other children. Yet they were very cathartic – excellent therapy. At first I had the impression that PLs were obligatory, so I resisted them, but then I overheard another kid saying how much he looked forward to them and I realised that I also liked them."

Like most others, Freer enjoyed the General Meetings. "And indeed I still enjoy meetings. They are an opportunity to have an interesting discussion – intellectually stimulating. You couldn't have the same discussions outside a meeting. In the General Meetings kids were intelligent and objective, whereas outside they were almost totally subjective. You were able to vote against your best friend if you felt it was right, without any feeling of having betrayed him, and with no hard feelings afterwards. Kids have that gift of being able to be totally objective, whereas in many of the cooperative meetings I've attended since adults behave extremely subjectively."

Like morality, democracy at Summerhill is caught rather than taught. "I enjoyed GMs long before I began speaking. They were enjoyable to observe. Many of the older kids were extremely impressive. There was one family in particular – four children all older than me, called Saunders – who were exceptionally sensible, and one hundred per cent reliable; everybody looked up to them for their doses of good sense. I used to use them as a gauge to measure the quality of an argument – particularly Mervyn Saunders."

The weekly Tribunal was, in Freer's case, particularly effective. "I was always being brought up. On one occasion Johnny Condon and I were caught stealing coffee and sugar from the pantry. We had been doing it for a long time before we were caught. The fine we got was that we should receive our own supplies of coffee and sugar every week until the end of term. Every week a large parcel was left outside the door of our room, and the funny thing was we began to feel so guilty about it that we asked for the 'punishment' to be rescinded. We felt we had been punished enough. It had a powerful effect on my thinking. I began to develop an intellectual awareness that things were not black and white; the human mind was complex. Johnny and I talked at great length about what was happening. We were eleven at the time."

Freer thinks this sort of thing should happen more often, in society in general. "It's necessary for kids to be told that even though they've done wrong people still love them. The heavy-handed approach is wrong and creates more problems. You have to separate the action from the person." Far from meting out savage retribution, in the manner of *Lord of the Flies* (where, it should be noted, the children came from authoritarian backgrounds) the Summerhill kids' punishments were, in Freer's opinion, always enlightened. "Most fines consisted of digging the garden or cleaning windows. When you received your punishment you just got on and did it without a feeling of guilt; it didn't change people's attitude towards you."

But there was one incident that incurred the wrath of the entire community. "A black girl had come to Summerhill from the U.S. at the same time as a white American boy from the Southern States. I suppose he had brought all his cultural baggage with him. Anyway, in an argument with her he called her a 'nigger'. Everyone was deeply shocked. Racism is an externally imposed value, which doesn't come naturally to kids. They had no experience of this sort of thing. They could only regard it as an extremely anti-social act. The boy was brought up at a Special Meeting and the strength of feeling expressed and the measures taken were so effective that he did change his opinion and even argued with his parents that they were wrong when he returned home." Summerhill, as Freer observed, simply doesn't allow those kinds of attitudes to prevail.

Stealing goes on at all schools, and particularly at boarding schools, but at Summerhill, Freer thinks, the children stole more for the challenge than for gain. "We used to hold contests to see how much each person could get away with. We did a whole series of raids on a nearby sweetshop. The owner kept constructing new defences, so we would devise new ways of outwitting him. One challenge was for each member of the gang to steal as much as he could wearing only a pair of swimming trunks and wellington boots." The success rate, Freer remembers, was very high. Nobody ever got caught. This is when the children were younger. In Freer's opinion most kids have grown out of stealing by the time they leave. This seems to bear out Homer Lane's assertion that most stealing by young children is a form of play. If it persisted into the later teens he called it 'misdirected social energy'.

Freer went on developing his practical skills. When he was 14 he and a friend started a business mending bikes for other kids. "We did this for about a term. I had a few special lessons in English with Harry, but I never did learn to read and write properly at Summerhill. I was in a minority; most kids did learn and most went to lessons in their later years."

At the age of 15, Freer was enjoying life and not considering leaving. "I'd never thought about it, but assumed I would stay on until I was 17. I'd long since stopped stealing, was very sociable and sat on all the committees. I remember receiving a unanimous vote to sit on the End-of-Term Committee – which was quite a prestigious thing – and I felt very good about that. It meant I was fully accepted by the community – and trusted." But one day Neill called him aside and told him there was nothing more that Summerhill could do for him. He wasn't studying for exams, as everyone else was, he was confident and capable and had overcome his problems. It was time to go. "I was extremely upset at the time," Freer recalls, "but in retrospect I feel it was a good decision."

After Summerhill

I had no idea what the outside world would hold in store or what job I would do. My dad had started a caravan-building business by then and I remember one of his drivers saying to me, "It's fine when you're there, but what happens when you leave?" I had discussed this with other people at Summerhill, but since we all knew former pupils who visited the school and had jobs we concluded that we'd be all right.

So I went back to Huntingdon to live in my dad's caravan. The outside world came as a huge shock: the attitude to life of people. A lot of their values seemed strange and twisted. I remember going to a Huntingdon palais with some local lads and being profoundly surprised and disturbed by their attitude towards sex and girls. Girls were slags who you scored with, and the easier they were to score the bigger the slag they were. They were simultaneously lusted after and despised. I found out that this was the prevailing attitude. My first job was putting up TV aerials, and there the talk was often about sex and girls, the same mixture of lust and contempt. But at Summerhill there was complete respect for women. Girls were the people you looked up to because of their greater maturity and skill at organisation. Sex was seen as healthy and good. Everyone was equally naive in a sense; there was a good deal of sexual experimentation but little intercourse. People sunbathed nude in the summer, but outsiders couldn't believe this. Whenever I mentioned it I was laughed at. The attitude was, 'This sort of thing simply doesn't happen at school.'

I think I have got a healthy attitude to sex, and this must largely be due to the openness towards sex and nudity at Summerhill. I also feel that my attitude towards sexual equality is genuine but light-hearted. I don't have much time for the heavy, politically-correct male attitude to women's rights. It strikes me as being insincere. In British schools of the early 60s there was still corporal punishment and segregation of the sexes. The atmosphere was authoritarian and repressive. Sex got mixed up with power. Working-class people in particular are very ambivalent about power. They both fear and respect it. For many, having power over women is the one expression of power they have. Summerhill on the other hand gives you power. You don't fear it. It gives you self-confidence and a feeling of equality. There is no dominant group or sex. You achieve influence by merit. It's full of individuals. No one group is powerful enough to create values, and that's partly to do with size. Summerhill would not remain the same if it grew any bigger.

Because I felt like an outsider at work, I withdrew from discussions with workmates because I wasn't confident enough to express my own opinions. At first I tried, but the other lads dismissed what I was saying as rubbish. I began to get the reputation of being a bullshitter. Whatever I told them about Summerhill they disbelieved. I found out that everyone had hated their schools. I was the odd man out. Saying you liked school made you peculiar. It had never occurred to me how bad other schools were. But I soon learned to stop talking about Summerhill. I feel I was a very naive kid: I had to learn to put up with the peculiar attitudes of the outside world, to mask my feelings. I don't think I ever have got over my feeling of horror at discovering what the outside world was like, but you learn to put up with it.

I spent a year working on building sites and became severely depressed because I didn't understand the environment I was in. I didn't actually realise my condition until one day my dad said, "Are you depressed?" I thought about it and replied, "Yes, I suppose that's what I am." So we discussed it and my dad thought it would be a good idea if I changed my environment for a while. The concept of hitch-hiking had been introduced to me by Wilf, who came to Summerhill as a gardener and later became a language teacher there. As a young man Wilf had hitched to Spain. So I bought myself a sleeping-bag and a rucksack and set off to hitch round England first as a trial run. Then I took what savings I had and travelled to Belgium. I was 16 and had no idea at the time that I was to spend virtually the next 10 years on the road and travel round the world twice.

I found that hitching was an interesting experience in itself: meeting people, being invited to stay with them. People fed me: they were generous and welcoming. In the first two months I visited Belgium, Holland, Spain, Portugal, France, Germany and Lapland. Then I went back to Holland and I still had £30 left, so without any clear idea of what I intended to do I returned to France. I arrived in one town in the middle of a jazz festival where I met a lot of other travellers. Some of them had been to Turkey, which sounded interesting, so I went there. And from there to India, South-East Asia, Indonesia. A little money went a long way. The £30 lasted me four months. In Kuwait I sold my blood for another £30, and whenever I needed money this is what I would do. I also began selling off what possessions I had, such as my watch and a pair of jeans. I discovered that watches could be bought cheaply in Kuwait and sold for a good profit in India. I made quite a lot of money from this enterprise. In Bombay I worked for a while as a film extra, which was well paid. In Laos I took a job in a U.S. Army storehouse.

I had visited over 100 countries when I decided to spend all my savings on a flight to Australia. I arrived flat broke, walked off the plane and got a job. However, I was so tired from travelling that I fell asleep and was sacked. But the next day I got another job. I spent a year in Australia, mostly working, and saved a lot of money. Also in Australia I at last learned to read and write, by teaching myself. My illiteracy had begun to embarrass me. Having to fill in visa forms at frontiers was an ordeal which I would bluff my way through. Also I was fed up with not being able to read billboards or road signs. Half the time I didn't know where I was going or what town I was in. In

Japan I'd taught English for a while – through conversation – but when someone asked me to write something down I couldn't oblige. I did make a bit of an effort to learn to read and write there, but it was not until I found myself living in a trailer in the Australian desert, whilst helping to build an aluminium plant, that I had the time and opportunity to get down to it. I bought a dictionary and a few books and within three months I was literate. I felt very good about that.

I was having a great time. Travelling the world and getting by had made me very confident. Most people I met seemed impressed with what I was doing and gave me excellent feedback. For six years I managed to avoid a single winter. As soon as the weather changed I would move on. This had the added advantage of meaning I could travel light. I often slept outside covered by only a thin sheet and wore nothing but a shirt and pair of trousers. I ate in cafés or at people's homes and slept in fields or, occasionally, if I felt like having a bath and a bed, a cheap hostel. I was never ill (although on my second world trip I did contract malaria).

The journey I undertook then would not be possible nowadays. You could hitch-hike through Iran, and virtually everywhere else, unimpeded. Today there are too many restrictions. In those days also travellers were rare, a novelty. Nowadays people are getting sick of them.

It was a very adventurous life and I was discovering places and events, not as a tourist, but by accident. For example I arrived in Rio de Janeiro just before the carnival. I was always stumbling across events and historic places like this, including what I later discovered to be major tourist attractions. I came across a building in India that I thought was wonderful. Years later I saw a photograph of it and discovered it was the Taj Mahal. I just went wherever I felt like going. Sometimes I forgot the names of my destination. I remember in Sweden some people stopping to ask me if they were on the right road to Stockholm and I couldn't tell them. I was sometimes put in prison for a night, for vagrancy, and once I was held for two weeks in South America on suspicion of being a member of Che Guevara's guerilla army.

In 1968 I wandered into Haight Ashbury in California and discovered a label for myself. I was a hippy. I enjoyed the atmosphere of California at that time, but I felt that a lot of hippies were trying to live through what I'd already experienced at Summerhill. I think I was a boring or square hippy. I liked smoking grass, which I'd been introduced to in Turkey, but I never drank alcohol or took LSD. Also I'd become used to going to bed early and getting up at dawn, whereas most hippies liked to talk and smoke late into the night.

Everywhere I went I saw copies of the US edition of *Summerhill.* When I mentioned I'd been there people believed me, in complete contrast to the reaction of people in England, and for the first time in years I was able to talk about it. I found the Americans of that period very open, receptive to new ideas. This was refreshing. They wanted to hear about Summerhill. I was treated as a celebrity and invited to give talks.

My first world tour ended in South America. After a three-day journey through Brazil I emerged, covered in red dust, at Belem, the last outpost on the Amazon before Guyana. I'd had no trouble with the absence of an entry visa before, but this time I was put in prison and ordered to be deported. In prison I met an American sailor who was waiting for his captain to collect him. He suggested that the captain might be able to offer me a job on their ship which was prospecting for oil. And he did. This got me off the deportation hook and for the next seven months I worked and saved several thousand dollars. At San Miguel I signed off and decided to go home.

It wasn't long before I was back on the road again, but my second world trip was interrupted with a prison sentence in Canada. I'd been caught on camera selling grass to undercover agents at a festival. This was ignored at the time but I was later stopped for speeding, taken to court and charged with both offences. I made the mistake of smart-assing the judge and wound up with a two-year prison sentence and a deportation order. I served nine months. Prison gave me the opportunity to think about my life and where it was going. I'd had a good time, but I was beginning to feel guilty about scrounging and living off other people's hospitality. I felt I must do something.

I arrived in London during the India-Pakistan war of the early 70s and volunteered to join 'Operation Omega', a non-violent direct-action peace initiative which was highly critical of Oxfam's involvement in the war. It was felt that by staying well away from the front line Oxfam was actually creating a refugee problem. Operation Omega wanted to get right to the heart of the war. Ten people, including myself and Satish Kumar, raised enough money to buy a couple of ambulances, drove out to the border between the two countries and stopped, right in the middle of the combating armies. Not only did we manage to stop the fighting for several days, but we also had a direct influence in changing Oxfam's future war-zone operations.

It was bizarre. Officers from both sides offered us tea and cucumber sandwiches and the same politeness and attention. They came from the same region and had attended Sandhurst together. All that separated them was an arbitrary line.

After the war there was an outbreak of cholera. I met a US doctor who had devised a simple oral medicine to replace the usual injections. We set up the 'Cholera Cure Unit', raised some money, recruited local student doctors and went into Bangladesh, driving from village to village and curing, swiftly and easily, thousands of people who would otherwise have died from dehydration. This lasted about a year.

After India I went to Africa for a while, then returned to England. In 1973 I set up the Lifespan community in Yorkshire with Hylda Sims. Lifespan was a therapeutic community modelled on Summerhill where people could come for a short or long stay to release their tensions. It set up a wholefood co-op and building business. There were kids as well as adults and a school was set up. I feel it was successful. The community even coped successfully with a heavy drinker; it voted to give him enough money to drink. There were four or five Old Summerhillians around. Some people stayed for weeks, others for years. There was plenty of space and an exhilarating climate on the moors, which I think contributed towards its success. I occasionally visit and find that it's very much the same as when we set it up. Like Summerhill it's preserved its culture.

I left because I wanted to become more politically active, to extend my range of interests. My next enterprise was to set up Beechwood College in Leeds for ICOM [Industrial Common Ownership Movement]. I found a big mansion, raised £200,000 from the Manpower Services Commission for its purchase and borrowed £30,000 from another source to renovate it and turn it into a training centre for co-ops. At weekends I ran it as a commercial conference centre to create an income for the training course. I ran this for five years, until 1985/86. I was working seven days a week and doing virtually everything, including running the bar. In the process I became worn out and my hair turned grey. I left it doing very well and it's still going.

Because of my experience running Beechwood I was able to set up in partnership as a freelance consultant for businesses and cooperatives. In the process I learned marketing and became a very good teacher. I was employed by the Plunkett Foundation to do training work overseas. Then I decided to take things easy for a couple of years.

My next job was to write a proposal for Action Research to look at community enterprises on housing estates, and as a result of this I set up Community Economy, another enterprise which is still going. I raised half a million pounds and employed 19 people to live and work on housing estates for a couple of years to see what could be done in the way of discovering potential for economic initiatives. I helped people set up credit unions and businesses which I monitored, producing an evaluation document after three years.

After this I helped set up the Land and Building Trust. This is a charity to which property is donated by a city or town council, on the understanding that it will be used for some socially beneficial project. I helped establish many training workshops on these sites. The Social Audit, which I developed, is used by several projects and businesses in this country. Running in parallel with the financial audit it deals with the environmental impact, social effect and objectives of an organisation. This adds an entirely new dimension to the concept of profit and loss.

When I got married I decided I needed a more stable career, and for the first time in my life applied for a full-time job. I became managing director of a commercial subsidiary of the Intermediate Technology Development Group, a branch of the Schumacher Institute, and managing director of a training centre in Stoneleigh for VSO [Voluntary Service Overseas]. So once again I found myself going all over the world, visiting developing countries as a consultant and frequently flying to New York to raise funds for projects from the World Bank and the United Nations. My brief was to help establish as many socially useful projects as I could, anywhere in the world. But now that I had two children I tried not to be away from home for too long.

Some years ago I set up the Friends of Summerhill Trust, at Zoë's invitation, and became its first secretary. I resigned from this, but continued as a member and helped to organise the summer workshops.

Summerhill has survived, I feel, because of the strength of its structure and organisation. Although it is fully democratic as far as its internal workings are concerned, it is supported by a hierarchical framework. At the top of the pyramid is the principal in whose hands the buck stops. Other progressive schools have failed because they have not grasped this principle. Cooperative managements have ended up squabbling amongst themselves, dividing into factions, and forgetting about the children whose interests they are supposed to serve. It is also of fundamental importance that the principal should be someone whose primary interest is not in teaching but in the functioning of the community. It will be a bad day for Summerhill if it ever falls into the hands of the teachers. Teachers can't help wanting to teach, it's in their nature, and it wouldn't be long before some lessons started to become mandatory. Summerhill is a therapeutic community more than a school. It's principally a response to bad parenting, which is actually getting worse. It's needed more than ever today. The great benefit of Summerhill is that you learn how to learn. Many people who have done well in formal education are stuck, but Summerhill offers you the skill to learn new tricks.

Postscript (2011)

I left the Intermediate Technology Development Group and freelanced for 10 years, working in various organisations. I have since become involved in Social Enterprise as a consultant, mainly working overseas, advising organisations on the development of enterprises that are run cooperatively by the people who work in them. My clients include Oxfam and the British Council to the EEC. I live with my wife near Hay-on-Wye.

Ethan Ames
1962~66

One of the criticisms that is levelled at current educational policy is its over-preoccupation with qualifications. This is not only an inhibiting factor in many people's development, where schooling assumes the ascendancy over education, but it can negatively influence a pupil's sense of self-worth. Ethan Ames, who was one of the first of the "new wave" of Americans to attend the school in the Sixties following the publication in the USA of 'Summerhill: A Radical Approach to Education', forged a highly successful career which was in no small degree enabled by the self-confidence and faith in himself that Summerhill engendered, despite his lack of higher academic qualifications.

Ethan Ames was born in 1949. His father, who came from a New England family, had moved to California to study composition with Nadia Boulanger and met Ethan's mother who was at drama school. Ethan was born in Washington State when his father was doing his army service. When he was about six months old the family returned to Santa Barbara. "In those days Santa Barbara was a very quiet, extremely beautiful little town with mountains on one side and sea on the other. There was a lot of freedom to play. There were lots of parks and everyone had big gardens and there was the beach, so it was nothing at all like living in a city."

Ethan went to a very free nursery school, then on to the local elementary school. "It was OK, but looking back I realise there were always bits that I hated about it. I couldn't sound my Rs or my Ss for quite a long time, so I remember having to go to developmental reading class which I loathed. But I quite liked a lot of the lessons, and history particularly. I read constantly. It wasn't until 6th grade (which is like the last year of English primary school) that I started disliking school quite a bit. Then I went on to Junior High and disliked a lot of it. I hated sports and it was a real sort of gung-ho regimented approach. It was so macho and I just wanted to spend my time with the girls. Also I was very into art and music and reading, so everybody thought I was a sissy. I had a terrible time from that point of view, and that was the excuse for coming to Summerhill."

Summerhill: A Radical Approach to Education had become a best-seller in America in the Sixties. "My parents had read it. I never talked to them about my dislike of school, but they obviously picked up on it. They could see the effect it was having on me. Apparently I was taking it out on my siblings, though I'm not aware of this."

The children were not told they were going to Summerhill. "It was very convoluted because they introduced it by saying we were going to England on holiday. We were going for a long six months and so we would have to go to school during the term time. That was the line we were fed." In fact Ethan's parents were splitting up. "I had no idea, but basically my mother was just running away to England to get as far away as possible. One of her closest friends was at RADA and she heard lots of things from him about the theatre scene in this country. So she decided that's what she wanted to do. It was exciting. Oh God, yes, I loved it. Because I was very interested in history and I loved the whole bit about kings and queens and medieval history. So I was extremely excited. I think we all were. Sean would have been 12 at the time and the twins, Alan and Alex, were 10. We all reacted in different ways to the idea of going. Alan instantly started rebelling. He used to do horrendous things to his teacher. Just amazing."

Ethan remembers the date they arrived in London. "February 15th, 1963, which was that really terrible winter. There was snow till the end of March. First time I'd seen snow in a city. We did a mammoth tour of the Tower of London. St Paul's, Buckingham Palace and all that in the first couple of days and then trekked out to Summerhill. I think my mother stayed a couple of days in Leiston and then came back to London and found a flat."

By that time the children had been briefed about Summerhill. "I'm sure the fact that there were no compulsory games pleased me, but lessons I didn't dislike, so I continued to go. I gave up maths, I think, after a term because Neill was teaching it. He was teaching it out of these 1930s text books and in America they had already started what was called New Math, so I didn't understand a word that he said. I recall him as being fairly unmoving as a maths teacher. His approach was, 'This is what it is and you have to work through it.' It was sort of unforgiving in that sense. But his essay class was a totally different thing. That was you being creative and he would help you read your stories. I still have some stories that I wrote from there. And he was a great story-teller himself."

Ethan's first impression of Summerhill was that it was incredibly derelict and rundown. "I couldn't believe it. Here I was coming from Southern California, where it never gets below 60 or 50, arriving in England covered in snow –and it wasn't melting – to this incredibly dilapidated old English schoolhouse. I was put in the Carriages where there was no heating in those days, no radiators, just the coal boiler in the central room. That heated the water and you just had to leave your doors open in the hope that some of the heat would get in there, which it never did. It was freezing. I remember sitting on my bed with my sister reading or writing letters, with duffle coats on and our feet under the blankets and mittens and everything. So it was a big adventure, but it was very strange, and uncomfortable. I think my mother was horrified. I don't think she could believe what it was like. The cold penetrated the whole school. You were always aware of it, always bundled up. Usually you congregated in the library or the sitting-room where they had coal fires. That was another reason for going to lessons, because they had heating. I think after that winter they put in radiators.

"It was also very weird living with that many people. That took getting used to. And sharing a room with someone you didn't know. I only shared a term and a half because my room-mate left in the summer and after that I always had a room on my own. Partly this was because Ollie, who was my housemother, said no one else could live with me. I don't know why. I loved Ollie, absolutely adored her. She was always happy and smiling and joking and she always supported what you did. She always seemed to defend you. I don't know whether it was just me or whether she did that with everybody. She was very eccentric and lived in a caravan out behind the tennis courts, separate from everybody else. Every evening she played her Frank Sinatra and Kid Ory records and practised her trombone. She'd been a pupil herself, years ago, and she was one of those people you couldn't age – like Ena. Ollie was a huge influence and so was Ena in a way, but one saw her much more as the headmistress. She was much more down-to-earth and pragmatic but also, I found, incredibly kind. And the two of them were probably the people who I looked up to most."

Ena's son, Peter Wood, who was to die tragically young of Weil's disease, was an important influence. "He was seen as a sort of younger father figure than Neill, whereas Neill was much more of a patriarch. This is the way I perceived it. I remember my mother saying when I needed to shave: 'Oh, go and speak to Peter, he'll tell you how to do it.'"

There were some very good teachers there, Ethan remembers, "but there was certainly not any kind of pressure at all to take exams. In fact I took three or four 'O' levels when I was 16 and I passed English. This really surprised me because I didn't like English, in fact, and I liked English Literature even less. Not because of the reading, because I loved reading the books, but I hated the analysis. I found it completely destroyed the books for me. And in English language I loved the vocabulary but the grammar bits I absolutely detested. I was very miffed when I passed English first time, rather than the subjects which I'd rather have passed. And the next year – I stayed till I was 17 – I don't think I took any exams. I jacked them in. Now I gather everyone at Summerhill takes exams. That would have been unheard of while I was there. I think it's the change in culture in the outside world. There's so much pressure that you can't work in bloody Boots without exams. Then it was more studying for its own sake. Because you enjoyed the subject. The thing was, if you're that kind of a person you obviously would draw out of the teachers as much as you could. And that would encourage them to give you more.

"There was a group of us there who were all Tolkien junkies and we all had nicknames from the book. I was one of the Nazgul – I presume because I was tall and thin and tended to wear black, but also because I was seen as someone who was fairly dour. I can remember having huge bouts of depression. I suspect it was about being 14/15 years old. Just that typical male teenage depression thing."

Theatre was another big influence. "I was very into Shakespeare. Not from reading but from seeing. My mother being an actress, every single holiday we would go to Stratford or London, and we were steeped in Shakespeare in that sense. I saw the famous Peter Hall *Wars of the Roses* with Peggy Ashcroft, Ian Holm and David Warner. It was astonishing. I can still remember it. It had a huge effect on me and even more made me adore history, certainly that period of history. We saw those early 60s Pinter plays – *The Homecoming*, I can still remember that. It was a bit above me, but I remember all the pauses and the sort of stiltedness, and I'm sure that had an effect on me. But it didn't seem abnormal because my parents had been in those things in America – they did all the Ionescos and Becketts. It was always avant-garde plays like *End Game*. Even if I didn't see them it all filtered through – Papa's in an ash can tonight. And I remember reading Ionesco at Summerhill – *The Bald Prima Donna* and stuff like that. Even when my mother had gone back to the States, my sister and I would always make a trip to Stratford and see everything that was on. And when I moved to London I went to the theatre constantly.

"We went to the cinema a lot. I remember seeing all those Ealing comedies, because the Leiston cinema was a real second-run house, although I do remember seeing Polanski's *Repulsion* there. But usually you went to Aldeburgh for art films. All of us loved going to the cinema, and because a lot of our parents lived in London, that created a social network outside of school as well. You did tend to stick with your immediate age group, slightly above and slightly below. Some half of them were American, half English. I don't remember any Europeans.

"The majority of Summerhillians I would say were from quite intellectual or artistic backgrounds, but there were a few who certainly didn't learn things but were still perfectly intelligent. On the other hand there were some who were totally anti-social and probably psychotic. One I remember used to recite Hitler's speeches and walk around in jackboots and he was Jewish, needless to say. I believe he sent a letter bomb to Peter Wood at one stage. I don't think Summerhill did anything for him. He was 14 when he came, I think. They should never have let him in. It was very unusual me going, because I was 13. Even then they tried not to accept people over 12. But because there were four of us, I was part of the package. I don't recall having any difficulty settling in. I certainly didn't rebel in an anti-social way. I did eventually rebel because I found I was being ostracised because I was perceived as Goody-Two-Shoes. I became an avid smoker."

Like Robert Muller, Ethan was around when Summerhill elected one of its periodic dictatorships, this time under the direction of the older students. "On the whole I'd say the General Meetings worked very well, but, and I gather it happens in any generation, there comes a point where it falls apart and breaks down. More and more people were breaking the school's laws; people weren't going to bed when they were supposed to, and no one was sticking to the rules. I can't remember what the other events were that led to it, but there was a complete deterioration. It had happened a couple of times while I was there, where they just dropped all the rules, except for the health and safety ones. You'd get these zombies walking around, because they'd stayed up till two in the morning. Usually what happened was you'd have a week of that and then people would say, 'Please bring back the bedtime laws.' Everybody had learnt the lesson that you needed to have rules and regulations. What happened this time was that it didn't improve. So a dictatorship was declared, and Albert Lamb was the dictator. Al was trying to prove something politically, that this is what it would mean if you weren't self-governing – the alternative was despotism. But it created a hell of a lot of bad feeling amongst a lot of people. It left a sour taste for a long, long time. The staff kept out of it. I certainly know that I sided with Al, because we felt we had to do something and make people understand the consequences. I think what brought it about was there was a lot of non-participation going on at this time. People weren't coming to the meetings. It was a very unpleasant, horrible period.

"There's one thing that Summerhill is not unique in. Kids acted like kids. So you will get 14- or 15-year olds going through the change of life and it will affect them in ways which Summerhill is not going to make any better. It isn't all sweetness and light by any means. You get people walking round in deep depressions and being antisocial or non-communicative – so it's no different in that sense. I think there were kids there who would have been better off in special schools. There probably is more of a realisation now about kids' psychological problems and the social effects it has than there was in the 60s. Sixties psychology was probably more psychiatry than psychology or sociology. There was a lot less looking at society in general. I think my brother Sean, who's become a psychologist, picked up on that."

After Summerhill

Summerhill didn't help me develop artistically because I was totally self-taught, but from a mental point of view it was very important. It gave one the freedom to develop and in a way it made one be successful. But it made it difficult to do what was asked of you when you went on a course afterwards. For instance, when I came to London it was fine being in a crammer, because I was just there to pass the exams. But I would keep writing about what I wanted to write about, rather than what they wanted to hear. And when I did A-level Art, I found it difficult to put up with the course work – I found it restrictive. In fact I failed A-level and only got an O-level.

What Summerhill did was give me the strength and belief to do what I wanted to do. When I went on to art college to do graphic design, having got five 'O' levels, the stipulation was I had to do 'A' level Art as well as the foundation course. I found that I was being very successful on the course, and getting on extremely well with the head of the course and several of the tutors, but I hated the 'A' level work, which was life-drawing and everything – mainly through lack of confidence because I think I'm a dreadful drawer and I hated everything to do with it.

In the end I said, "I'm not going to these classes, they're pointless." The poor teacher was beside herself and said, "Well you have to do it." And went screaming and yelling to the head of department. I said, "Look I don't need to do this, I'm the best student in the class – it's totally unnecessary." And the head of department said, "Just let him get on with it." As it turned out, I *was* the best student on the course. My inability to draw had nothing to do with the fact that I was going to be a good graphic designer. So Summerhill very definitely helped me to do that. It gives the confidence to do what you want to do.

Because Summerhill gave me the freedom to be highly creative, it really gave me the reason for going into graphic design. I was on the End-of-Term committee every year, which was always on a theme – creating a theme for the end-of-term party – and graphic design is very much about solving briefs. It's not about just being creative. Here's a problem, okay, solve it. That's what graphic design is. So it did follow through very much from that, though it was totally unconscious, but looking at it retrospectively, that was the origin.

After foundation I went on a three-year vocational graphic design course at the same college – East Ham Technical College. They didn't have BA then, they had diploma. While I was still there I got a holiday job at the BBC. That's how I got into television graphics. I really loved doing that and at the end of the second year the BBC offered me a full-time post as assistant graphic designer. I turned it down because I wanted to finish college. I wanted to major in TV graphics, which no one did at that time. College said, "We don't do it," and I said, "That's all right, I'll give you the projects, you just write the brief for me." So to all intents and purposes I designed my own course. Everything was done by hand in those days, because it was before computers. It was a nightmare, but very inspiring and challenging.

I was aware that other students had a much more deferential attitude towards the tutors. I felt much more mature. In many ways I had a closer affinity with the lecturers than with the students, which was maturity in the sense of dealing with other people. That's obviously to do with Summerhill because it's about living with other people, accepting them for what they are. Working as part of a team very much comes from Summerhill. Everything I have done in my career is always work as part of a team. I hate working on my own. Now I don't think that's a Summerhillian trait. There are certain Summerhillians who like working on their own, because Summerhill equally gives lots of people the ability to be completely independent. Certainly it has produced artists who work totally on their own.

After I completed my college course, I taught graphic design for five years at the same college. Initially I'd gone freelance. The BBC wouldn't employ me because I'd turned them down, and also I think because I was living with Julia, my future wife, who was also working at the BBC, and they had a thing about people living together and working together in the same department. In the first year I was freelancing, the head of department at college asked me back to do part-time lecturing, which within a year built up to being full-time. That was odd because I was the third-year lecturer for people who had been in their first year when I was in my third. It took a bit of winning their confidence, but it worked out very well.

I loved teaching. The only reason I gave it up was I was getting out of touch with what I was teaching. I threw myself totally into my work, so consequently I didn't do any graphic design, or very little. I decided I wanted out because I didn't feel I should be teaching when I didn't know what I was teaching. I didn't want to become an old fuddy-duddy professor. That's the danger with teachers only being professional teachers – they lose touch with what they're supposed to be teaching. The advantage I've found with vocational courses is that students I've seen from the point of view of wanting to employ people are often much better prepared than people from BA courses. BA students have had so much theory and pontificating thrust upon them that that's all they think about.

Summerhill did give me an advantage in relating to the students. There are several advantages which would have been there irrespective. One was that I was virtually their age, so there's a lot in common anyway. But, having been to Summerhill, that whole hierarchy thing just is not there. I felt much more a part of them, a part of their team, than they would expect. Part of what you have to do therefore is gain their confidence, because they find it very peculiar. They've never come across that. They expect you to be a teacher, and to be separate. So it is quite a challenge to get over that. But it's incredibly rewarding to both sides, and that's what I really loved about teaching. You really did become part of a team. I would have this argument with some of the people I'd gone to college with because they'd say, "Why the hell are you there teaching? a) it's the bloody place you went to and b) it's such a waste because you were one of the best students; you should be out there working, making a name for yourself." My attitude was that I was being just as creative, if not more, working with these students, as I would be in a design group. Because I like working with people. That's why it doesn't bother me now being completely a manager, because I'm being creative with people. It doesn't bother me in the slightest that I don't have to do another piece of graphic design, because I'm working with people being creative. And that's a buzz.

I think in my management style I have taken over some of that feeling of being on the same level. It was very interesting when I applied for my current job because my only qualifications are five 'O' levels and a Licentiateship to the Society of Industrial Artists & Designers. The majority of managers at the BBC are university graduates. But the person who is my boss had heard of Summerhill. The head of personnel was concerned about my lack of qualifications, whereas my boss said, "That doesn't bother me. I can see what he's like. I can see how he deals with people, and he is going to have to control a hundred people, and it's immaterial what his academic qualifications are." Thank God someone was on the panel like that. It shows you can be valued for what you bring in dealing with people and their relationships.

Now I am a manager of a large department I find I have to step back slightly. You have to be slightly distanced to be able to wield the authority. People can't take that kind of thing if they are in a very personal relationship with you. When I was a manager at TVam, which was a smaller department, I used to have huge dinner parties at home. On our days off we'd go out into the country. I don't do that at all now with staff. I do have huge regrets about that because it does make it much more of a loner kind of role. You do have to make some pretty horrendous decisions. The first three months in the present job I had to make about 12 people redundant. You can't do that if you're on a personal-relationship basis with people. That's where Summerhill is at a disadvantage – because it's only 60 people at a time, or whatever, on the same wavelength, thinking together. And then you go out into the big, bad world where everybody doesn't think like you, so you must change. But at the same time Summerhill makes you flexible and tolerant, so you can adjust.

I genuinely believe that I'm not competitive. I am obviously somehow competitive to have gotten to be head of graphics at BBC TV, but I've not set my sights on that. I have not gone out and stepped on people and done the best pushing myself. I can't sell myself at all. That's why I didn't go anywhere near advertising. The thought of selling anything, let alone myself, is foreign to me. I'm sure that's Summerhillian. But someone always has to make unpleasant decisions. I was talking to my mother about it while I was at TVam. It was something where I had to make a decision and it made me really unpopular with people who were close friends. I was finding it very difficult to deal with and she said, "Look, even in a democracy you have a president. Someone has to make the final decision." So at Summerhill, Neill or Zoë, whoever it is, has to make that ultimate decision. They're in a lonelier position because of it.

You were aware that Neill had the final responsibility for who was sacked and who was taken on. You also suspected that Ena had a say in it. She was very much the power behind the throne. There were a couple of things where you knew it was very definitely Ena who made the decision. There was a teacher who was sacked – it was after I left, I believe. He had a boyfriend, and they were living together at Summerhill, and the story went that Ena sacked them because they were gay. One version was she didn't agree with homosexuality, the other was that she felt they had to go to protect the school.

I don't know what Neill's attitude was towards homosexuality. The only evidence I have is what is in the book, and through talking to other people who were there. The impression I got was perfectly tolerant but very old-fashioned. It was still an illness attitude towards it. Bad conditioning. The main thing which did rile me was his statement that Summerhill had never produced a homosexual. I couldn't understand why he'd say that, because a) how in the world would he know? b) what a presumption. Equally, what one doesn't know is how much he was saying that to protect himself and the school. I can totally understand it would be the worst thing in the world to get out.

When I was there the policy was that you shouldn't be sleeping together if you were straight, let alone gay, because there was a huge fear of there being a pregnancy. It would be instant shutdown. So, even the idea of straight sex was very cloak and dagger. I don't think there was much sex. It was very openly discussed, because it was the Sixties, the free-love generation crap. The politicisation of sex was discussed, the philosophy that it was good, it should be open, and there was nothing to be embarrassed about over any kind of sex. Of course in practice none of it held a bit of water, because that isn't how people acted. I don't think it would make any difference how open you were or how much a society may change, it will always be a thing of embarrassment between teenagers or children, because it's part of growing up. You don't understand it. There was a huge embarrassment about masturbating or admitting that you did. I remember in the Carriages, when you'd go to bed, you'd get people calling across the corridor: "Are you having a wank?" You'd say, "No," and they'd say, "You don't know what you're missing." Or you'd say "Yes," and they'd say, "You revolting, dirty person." So there was all that teenage macho stuff. It was no different from anywhere else.

I'm sure I did have feelings about being gay but you can only tell retrospectively. I probably knew I was gay when I was eight, or ten. God knows. You only realise that when you think, Oh, yes, I was always much more interested in looking at the teenage brothers of my playmates than their sisters. Certainly I was much more aware of being excited by seeing boys or men naked, when I was a teenager, than women. But I would never have admitted it. I wasn't grown up enough. Even the Summerhill teachings had not given me the strength to say, "Oh, right, I'm gay, and that's OK." It was, "Shit, I wonder if I'm gay." I had three girlfriends when I was at Summerhill and I slept with one of them once. Absolutely terrified, both of us, because we didn't use contraception. I would never have admitted to being gay at Summerhill and I can't imagine anyone doing so, because, although in all the discussions about it it was taken to be an OK thing, it was a very condescending point of view that was taken.

I didn't come out, or admit I was gay, till 1976. By which time I had a daughter. I'd had an affair with a man, but my wife and I decided it was a phase, because I wasn't willing to admit to being totally gay then – if you can say that anything is total. It was only after having my daughter that I realised I was still intensely attracted to men and the feelings were getting stronger. In the end I went to a gay club with my brother who was over from the States – because Alan is gay as well, and he'd been out a good couple of years. And I think Alan in a way was a catalyst because he was saying, "You can pull yourself together. Stop being such a fool." It was no surprise at all to me that Alan was gay, and it certainly wasn't from his point of view that I was. I think he knew more probably than I did or was willing to admit.

I'm on perfectly good terms with my wife and always kept up the relationship with my daughter. When she was in her teens she virtually lived with me full-time, because she could get to school and later college easily. She knew I lived with a man and that we slept in the same bed, but she probably didn't know what that meant till she was 13 or 14. She may have had some problems with that, but it's not apparent. Certainly the boyfriends she's brought home have been aware of the situation and have seemed to be perfectly comfortable with it. So she's obviously learned how to explain it to people. She would have had divided loyalties between her parents, but no more than if I'd been living with another woman. She did, obviously for a long time like any child does, hope that her parents would get back together again. Just as she has had to learn to have relationships with people who accept I'm gay, I can't have a relationship with someone who can't tolerate me having a child. So it's again about tolerance, and accepting that people are different.

I would defend Gay Rights up to the hilt, but I didn't go on marches. It is similar to not going on Aldermaston marches when we were at Summerhill, although we were all ban-the-bombers. It's about feeling that you don't have to stand up and scream and yell about it. I don't hide being gay from anybody, and occasionally I will make it blatantly obvious, for effect. But I don't constantly ram it down people's faces.

The problem that one has in society of any kind is understanding to be tolerant of other people and understanding that people are different. The majority of people disagreeing or not accepting things is through lack of knowledge and understanding. What's important about being able to teach in schools that homosexuality is normal or acceptable – or that there is absolutely nothing wrong with it and so people shouldn't be afraid of it – is not so that teenagers immediately start having gay sex. It's so that they can develop not having that fear. They probably won't have gay sex till after they've left school anyway. But they won't have gone through that period of being told. "This is wrong." Or it being hidden from them so they can't find out any information about it until they've left school.

In that sense Summerhill did help me to be gay with a lot less turmoil. Because, even in its very backward and cackhanded way of saying, "It's all right to be gay" – even if it was still unacceptable – it meant that, come the crunch, when I did decide, I wasn't suicidal about it. I have met people who've been absolutely terrified about admitting to being gay, and lots of people who've never told their parents they are gay. I do have a gay consciousness, and yet part of me feels, Well, why does it matter in the slightest? Yet again one does – and I don't know whether it's for support because you are ostracised, but one does tend to show a very direct interest in gay culture and want to keep aware of that kind of thing. I think it is because you have been pigeon-holed in this way. You know, it's the only area where you can totally expect the same kind of feelings without being questioned or misunderstood. Like feeling that if you're black you have to mix with black people. You are interested in how other people who are like you think, and what kind of empathy you may have with them. But I find more and more that I couldn't give a fuck about them, because they are as different as anybody. And why should they be the same, just because they're gay? None of us seem capable of saying, "Anybody can be anything and it doesn't matter." Even Summerhillians can't say that.

I see very few Old Summerhillians. When I do see them we still relate, we share a lot of memories. But we are equally very aware of our differences. Certainly more than, say, two years after we'd left. That happens with age. I'm much more aware of my differences with my brothers and sister.

The last time I went to Summerhill was maybe seven or eight years ago when they had one of the first Summerhill Society weekends. The only reason I didn't take anyone with me was because I wasn't living with anyone at the time. But I would have had no compunction about it. Indeed, my brother Alan took his lover. There wasn't any reaction, but Alan felt that there was still not enough open recognition that there had been gay people at Summerhill and that it was perfectly natural to be gay. This was when they were doing their heavy promotion drive and Alan said he would be more than happy to do promotion for Summerhill if they would accept that Summerhill did produce gay people. I think Zoë was rather shocked at this. And I think understandably a bit miffed because it was, "Well, if you do this I'll do that." I'm much less extreme than Alan is. Equally, I would hate to think that they were denying it still. Would I write a letter to *The Times* that they were still perpetuating this myth? I probably would actually.

Summerhill has changed and I wouldn't expect it to be the same. Of course it's going to be different, because the bloody world's different. And I don't think I'd want it to be the same. There's a hell of a lot I would hope to God is different from when I was there. Like the fact that people have a better awareness of the psychology of children. You'd hope they were more picky. This is the horrible business side of things – the realisation that if you're going to make something successful, and keep those things that are of value to it, you can't take kids who were rejected by every school going. If you take a reject they're going to be detrimental to you as well.

I did think about whether I would want to send my daughter to Summerhill. My whole attitude all along was that I didn't see it as necessary to make a decision unless events occurred where she was unhappy with what she was doing. The whole thing about Summerhill is to be happy in what you're doing. The only reason I was sent was because I was unhappy with my school. She was happy at her school, so why change it? She had a circle of friends. Why wrench her away from that just to send her to a school which you may think is better? If I felt she was being brainwashed, or if I radically disagreed with the policy of the school, I would change the school. But I didn't find anything wrong with it. I told her what I felt, so she had a diversity of information. Summerhill needs to be there to show that way to other people – that's what's important about it.

What Summerhill represents to me is tolerance. It's always the main word I come back to. Tolerance of your situation, tolerance of other people. The realisation that you can do something about the way you live, but you can't change the world. I can do my little bit, or I can shut up and just get on with life. A lot of people think I'm crazy. What's the point of worrying? There's nothing I can do. Just get on with your life and enjoy things. Tomorrow is another day. I've been fired; I've been made redundant twice now. It's not the end of the world. OK, I'm privileged, I've been lucky, whatever. I can't say that to a miner or somebody else and them believe me. But, if you believe it, if you have that philosophy, "Tomorrow is another day", and if you're tolerant and let things happen – life goes on.

Postscript (2011)

After five years as Head of Graphic Design, I left the BBC in 1999 and returned to teaching Design for Moving Image at Ravensbourne College of Design in South London. I was going back to school. I still find that my experiences at Summerhill colour my whole attitude towards teaching. You get the best out of your students if you treat them as equals. The feeling of continuity is exciting…and weird. I've taught the son of someone I taught when I first started teaching, and I've taught someone who also went to Summerhill – *and* who is openly gay!

I am still living blissfully happy with my partner Robert. We entered into a civil partnership in 2009, after 21 years together, taking the surname Chapman-Ames.

My daughter Tacita is married and has provided us with a grandson, who is now five. Tacita works in New York as a fashion designer for Calvin Klein and she sometimes employs my brother, Alan, who is still knitting. My sister Alex is living in the family home in California and has two grandchildren. Sadly, my brother Sean died in 2003. However, his daughter, Zoë, is close friends with Tacita and my sister's sons.

Since the original interview in 1996 a lot has changed and a lot has stayed the same. Re-reading what I said then, I don't think I would change any of it. It is, after all, a snapshot in time. If anything, I'd say in the current educational climate that I'm more pro-Summerhill. Whilst we may not have been required to attend lessons, we learned more academically than students in state schools do now! I'd like to think I have mellowed a lot and am less opinionated; however, I suspect everyone I know would say I'm getting to be even more of a grumpy old man!

Danë Goodsman
1962~72

The preconception that, with its policy of non-compulsory attendance at lessons, Summerhill could never produce anyone literate, let alone an academic, is belied, yet again, by the example of Danë Goodsman who, having been both a pupil and teacher at Summerhill, gained a PhD in the philosophy of education – her doctoral thesis, significantly, was on Summerhill. Subsequent to my interview with her, I met an American teacher who had stayed at Summerhill in the Sixties, and recalled Danë as someone who had made a marked impression on him with her ability to penetrate to the heart of the matter and ask precisely the right questions – in his words: a remarkable child-philosopher.

Danë Goodsman is, so far as I know, unique in that both her mother and her own children went to Summerhill. Danë was practically born into Summerhill having first gone there at 10 days old when her mother returned as a houseparent after separating from her father. Then, when her mother remarried, they lived on a farm about 12 miles down the road. "We were regular visitors," Danë recalls. "Ena had practically brought up my Mum, so it was like visiting granny really."

Danë began attending the local primary school, but did not find it very enjoyable. This was partly because she had to make a two-mile cycle journey there every day "and that used to get me down. To this day I don't like travelling to work. As far as the culture went it seemed like another kind of life, but nothing that bothered me particularly." Though she learnt to read easily, and had no struggle with school work in general, she feels that in some ways she must have seemed a bit of an oddity. "Not being frightened of grown-ups and all that stuff. Because I'd lived in Summerhill as a tiny child I think I was just used to being a person."

In Danë's opinion it was older children coming to Summerhill for the first time who tended to be full of trepidation, whereas those who started young, providing they came from secure backgrounds, found it easy. "They didn't really think about it. I think Neill's theory about the homesick child being the one who is unhappy at home is right. If you've got a very strong, happy, loving family you probably wouldn't even look back. I know that my children are feeling all right when they pay me no attention at all."

At first Danë spent most of her time with children who were younger than her. "Whether that was a reaction to having come from a mainstream school and having to find my feet, I don't know. I needed to start again. I don't know how long that lasted." Danë went to lessons when she was young. "I think all the little ones tend to. It's the place to congregate and all sorts of interesting stuff happens, though I couldn't tell you what we did."

In addition to Neill and his two wives there are a handful of other long-serving adults who assume almost mythic proportions in Summerhill's history. Such a one was Ulla Otte who stands out in Danë's and others' minds as both a consistent person and an excellent needlework and craft teacher. "Ulla's place was always open in the afternoons when the other lessons had finished, and I was interested in that stuff. It's stood me in such good stead because when I finished training to be a teacher I was about the only person in my group who could do all the practical things like basketwork, weaving, dressmaking. You name it, we'd done it with Ulla." Danë remembers Ulla's classes as always being a mixture of girls and boys – another expression of the sexual equality that obtained at Summerhill. "I don't think I ever felt any sense of male or femaleness in what you did until I left school. Long after in fact." She recalls that the most talented kids in Ulla's classes were Ethan Ames and his brothers and sister. "The Ames boys could sit there and knit you an Arran sweater out of their heads. They were just amazing. They'd come up with the most fantastic ideas and carry them out and they were always beautiful. The Ames family put on a puppet show which was just exquisite. They did everything: made the theatre and the puppets, wrote the script. It makes you sick!"

Danë remembers Ena as "a hell of a presence for everybody," a powerful person, capable and energetic with great organisational skills. She could also be quite frightening. "She used to call a spade a spade and that can be daunting. But young kids can take it, you see." Neill on the other hand, though remembered vividly, was not an integral part of one's day-to-day existence. "As far as I was concerned he was the guy who you asked if you wanted to cut down a big bough off a tree or something like that." Danë would read his fan mail which she found "a hoot. He used to get a stack of post every day. And he had a cuttings service. That was my favourite thing." Every day Neill would get cuttings from different parts of the world which, Danë feels, served two purposes for him. "In a way it was a vindication of what he was doing and also it was a way of keeping tabs on what was happening."

Danë stresses that Neill was not remarkable to the children. She used the same phrase as many Summerhillians: "He was just Neill." Neither was Summerhill felt to be remarkable. "It was just where we lived. I had no sense of this being other. I didn't learn any of that until I'd left school." Danë liked to spend her Saturday afternoons sitting and listening to Neill give his talks to the visitors. This was at a time when the school would get many more times the number of visitors than there were children in the school. "They came from all over the world to see Mr Neill. And every week they'd ask the same questions and he'd answer in the same way. I didn't think it was remarkable. It was what Neill did." Danë used to sit in because she was curious to see what these grown-ups wanted to know and she found it interesting that they would always ask the same questions.

"I don't think I realised what a wit and raconteur he was until I was much older. The only time I can remember laughing at a speech he made was at Zoë's wedding. He gave a bloody good speech. Very funny." But though a gifted public speaker, Danë found that his qualities did not translate well into the medium of television. "It was such a shame. He was too clever for his interviewers to understand him." Perhaps this goes part way to explaining why Neill's philosophy has not been given the serious attention that many think it deserves.

Danë enjoyed Neill's stories. "But what I remember that was really fun was spontaneous acting. We used to make plays up and Neill used to do a play occasionally. There was one about a gang the police had infiltrated and actually it turned out that the whole gang was made up of police, which got higher and higher up the rank. I remember him standing at the back of the theatre saying, 'Speak up, speak up, I can't hear you.' That was his idea of direction."

Teachers stood out for all sorts of reasons. "Good people and crazy people. Summerhill attracts the same number of crazies as everywhere else; it's just that as a child there you're allowed to say it out loud instead of having to suffer it in silence like most schools." There has always been a high turnover of staff at Summerhill, the principal reason being the poor pay. "If you want to do normal things like have a home and a family you can't really sustain it in Summerhill. So it's not really a good measure how long teachers stay there." Some Summerhillians have been more critical of the standard of teaching than others. In Danë's opinion "there have been plenty of damn good teachers there. Some people say the teaching went off in the Sixties, but I was there then and I went to all the lessons. Some people get bored and there's always plenty of other stuff to do, but my main interest has always been in books, so lessons were up my street." She was, as she says, a bookish child. "I basically read my way through the library. It was quite a surprise to me, when I went on afterwards, the number of things I'd read already that other people were about to read. One book I really loved was *The Catcher in the Rye*. I thought that was brilliant. It was just so clear and direct; shooting from the hip. And the frequent use of the word 'crap': it wasn't to shock or show off, it was just absolutely the right word to describe what was going on."

Television was a comparatively late arrival at Summerhill, children of previous generations having voted to keep it out. However, the 'plug-in drug' did not have the catastrophic effect that some feared it would. This might suggest that excessive TV-watching amongst children is as much a symptom as it is a cause of boredom and passivity. As Danë recalls, "Thursday night was the one night that the whole school watched the telly – *Tomorrow's World, Top of the Pops, The Man from Uncle*. But that was more or less it."

Apart from books, dancing ("I still love a good *throsh*, as we say in Norfolk") and art were Danë's principal interests. She later took a B.Ed in art. Here it is interesting to note the different effect of teaching styles on different children and in different times. Though art teacher Harry Hering's non-intrusive approach suited pupils like Léonard Lassalle, for Danë and her contemporaries he was uninspiring. "Then, when I was about 13 or 14, a chap called Robert Jones came to Summerhill – and he was brilliant. A really great teacher. A whole troop of us did art and several kids from that section are still doing art. One of the things about Summerhill is, if you are a teacher there, if you actually do something, then people join in. He himself would do a lot of drawing and that's the inspiration." Danë has been influenced by this approach in her own career as a teacher. "If I wanted the kids to do something, I'd do it myself. That way you have a dialogue because you're sharing the experience."

As Hylda Sims pointed out, many of the better teachers at Summerhill were comparatively formal in their methods. Robert Jones taught perspective at a time when state schools, and art colleges, were encouraging 'freedom of expression'. "Up to that point nobody had ever said, 'Well, actually, there's a formal way of doing this and we could teach you in an afternoon.' All this stuff about kids, be free, let them do their own thing and they'll develop in their own way – this is fine, but you get to a point where why should you keep re-inventing the wheel? So he taught us all to draw." Many of his pupils went on to gain degrees in art. When Danë went on to do a foundation course in art she remembers the head of department who interviewed her as being extremely impressed with her drawing. "For me it was just kind of ordinary, but for him of course most of the kids he was seeing couldn't really draw. They'd never been taught."

Teaching in the upper forms at Summerhill, Danë recalls, was more akin to university tutorials than school classes. "In lessons you might talk about something or other, then you'd go and bone up in your own room. If you had to know something in particular, you didn't need to waste time in the classroom doing it." What kept Danë going to lessons was being with other people, the social aspect. "Chatting about stuff, you know, having a common task. It was a good social occasion. I liked doing things like reading a play as a class. You'd share things in a different way and you'd reflect on things in a different way."

Another pleasure was being read aloud to as a class – the shared enjoyment of a story. One teacher read her way through the Greek mythologies. Whilst the story was being read the children would draw or knit. This practice continued into 'O' level study. "You'd be knitting to Shakespeare while everybody else was reading. Then it would be your turn and, funnily enough, when you picked your knitting up again you'd remember it all. Somehow, because you were actually doing that activity when you were listening, it brought back the whole thing. It's really peculiar." Other educators, such as Rudolf Steiner, have emphasised the close connection between memory – and the enhancement of linguistic and numerical skills – and practical skills such as knitting and sewing. In Summerhill this seems to have happened spontaneously.

Danë's main sport at Summerhill was riding. "It sounds terribly *Malory Towers*, so privileged. I used to take my own ponies back with me at the beginning of each term because Zoë had her stables there. And I rode in the holidays because we lived on a farm."

The Summerhill experience has profoundly shaped Danë's attitude to the arts, particularly film, theatre and novels. "I have a problem with novels and stuff which doesn't resonate with any kind of life that I recognise; where they seem to create tension by people not telling people things. That drives me completely barmy. That isn't anything to do with my life. My life is you just tell people and they tell you and you live in this front life instead of this kind of back life. I've seldom enjoyed theatre and I've always wondered why. I've come to the conclusion it's because it's the lie. These people really aren't saying that. They're actors. I find it very difficult to suspend my disbelief. The only time I can get involved in a play is when it doesn't really matter who's saying it because it's what they're saying that's interesting." As for example in Sartre's *In Camera*. "That was one of the first plays I enjoyed because it didn't matter who; it was the ideas. The same with Shakespeare. I think that if I had to describe myself – and that doesn't sound too grand – I think that is what I'm about: ideas."

It seems common amongst Summerhillians that by the age of 16 or 17 they are ready to spread their wings, so the transition to the wider world is welcomed. Summerhillians do not want to remain free children for ever. As Danë said, "Towards the end of my time there I used to get tremendously bored. I was well ready to leave. I'd done it – been there, worn that T shirt, caught that bus. I wanted a bigger world."

After Summerhill

I didn't discover philosophy until I was at university, doing my B.Ed., and it almost was an accident really. We had to put down various options for our final year, and I happened to go along to this philosophy lecturer's brief. I found it so vivid; I still remember it all. Not necessarily the content but I remember the room. It must have been late afternoon because I remember a shaft of sunlight and you could see all the dust swirling in it, and we were talking about – I guess it must have been relativism because she was saying, "Right, you're in the desert now, what's worth more, gold or water?" And just that simple notion made me think, yes, what we do is explainable in those terms. And we can take things apart and look at them inside. Because, of course, coming from Summerhill, I was very used to living in a totally up-front moral environment – you know, what I do affects other people and I know it; and I must respond to them because I've affected them. It was really exciting. I suddenly thought, I can bloody do this. I'm interested in this. Having gone through the motions – I mean I went into teaching slightly at odds with my tutors. What they were saying about kids wasn't from my understanding, and I assumed it was because I didn't know and I'd gone to that funny school, that dreadful school. It wasn't until I got philosophy that I could suddenly turn around and say, "That only works if this is your premise. If your premise is *this*, if you see the world *other*, like I do – 'like what I do'"… Suddenly I had the tools. Philosophy was the tool that I needed to express myself. So I did it as a major part of my final year and I've gone on with it ever since. I was awarded my PhD in 1993.

At the moment, to put it simply, I'm training the trainers of doctors – teaching them some of the theory of education. Eventually I hope to work directly with postgraduates, house doctors, senior house doctors – because doctors are in the position of having to learn new stuff all the time, just to keep abreast. And they are also a population under siege by their own training procedures. So I'm hoping I'll get a chance to get in there and see what they really do, and try and do different, as they say in Norfolk, because the way they learn is inefficient; they're wasting a lot of time. For example, if they're only learning stuff because their consultant might ask them, and then promptly forgetting it, that's not very useful to them – if they're finding themselves swamped, so that they're not really learning anything at all. This is the reality of being a trainee doctor. Whereas the image you're presented with is to be terribly successful.

Efficiency is rather a mechanistic word, so probably a better way of putting it is to say I want them to learn to their own satisfaction. I've always been interested in how people learn. I can remember as quite a little kid helping one of the other kids to learn her alphabet. I spent quite a lot of time working with her on that – inventing things and trying them out on her, poor girl. I was just fascinated by it.

After Summerhill I went to art school, just because I could do it. I'd always been so able in art it seemed the natural thing to do. But I was never really committed. I never had a question to answer in art. I could just do it. I don't think I did particularly well and I didn't get a place to do a BA, so I thought, "Oh, what in the bloody hell am I going to do?" I applied to clearing and these teacher training places came up. I went up to teacher training college about a fortnight before the new term and they gave me a place then and there. And that just suited me down to the ground. I was back to what I was interested in – which is how people learn. So I was lit up really, just by luck.

The degree was in two halves, the art side and the education side. And very quickly for me the education side was much more interesting. Because I was very skilled at art, I could tick along with it with no problem at all. This was 1975, and I just, as it were, hit the edge as Neill and Holt were going out of favour; were no longer part of any required reading list. But of course all my tutors would know about it. I think I was asked to speak about Summerhill once in the whole time I was there. I was quite shocked and amazed to discover that the college considered itself very right on, whereas as far as I was concerned it was 'Dinosaurs roam here.' But from my point of view most educators of any generation are weird. They don't really understand anything about children and how could they? They've never seen any real children. They've only ever seen kids who've gone through crazy places they call schools.

My first practice was in a rather *naice* primary school in Dulwich. The thing I remember from that was, the first time that I was allowed to dismiss the children at the end of the day I just said, "Right, that's it then, we're finished." And somebody could have died at the door with these kids rushing to get out. I'd never encountered people behaving like animals – because they had always been told to go table by table; the quietest table first and all that. So that shocked me. It always shocked me being called 'Miss'. The way we were treated in the staff room was amazing. You had to call them 'Miss' and whatever their name was. Obviously colleagues were called by their first names, but we were students. But I didn't mind that. I felt more comfortable, actually, calling them that. It sort of distanced you.

The second practice I did was in New Cross. That was a seriously tough secondary school. They'd only just had students back in because they'd had such a lot of violence against the teachers. But in fact of course it wasn't all tough; the kids were great and it was fine. Kids react violently to violent things, whether the violence done to them is physical violence or whether it is oppression of another sort. Obviously if you're a student they try it on. I remember being in the art room, and my supervisor was in there sitting behind these couple of lads, and they said to me, "Miss, what does masturbate mean?" So I said, "Playing with yourself." I wasn't going to go into lurid details and I wasn't not going to answer them. They just wanted to see how I'd react.

I think what kids look for is a level of honesty. Sometimes it's to do with being quite outgoing, although many successful teachers are quite shy – there's plenty of those about. I think people who are interested in other people, you know, genuinely interested in them – that comes across. But what most teachers spend most of their time dealing with is lack of interest in the subject. That's what causes most of the trouble.

I'd always known other schools were not as Summerhill, but what you didn't know was what that actually meant. When you're a kid, and you talk to other kids, you don't have any sense necessarily of standing in their shoes and feeling what they feel when an adult comes towards them. And that took me a long time to get a grip on. It has a kind of fairytale quality to it. You know, it happens out there somewhere. But to actually get a real understanding of that took me a while. I couldn't honestly believe that people would really react like that. With fear. That human beings, just from the position they had, could make them frightened. I'm frightened of people who physically threaten me, but no power position in the world would frighten me. You might say that with a lot of kids they don't feel fear, it's resentment. But resentment is a kind of fear. A reaction to fear.

Fear in terms of learning is the most common emotion you come across. Not just in schools. Anywhere. To anybody. Anyone learning anything. Fear is the biggest single emotion involved in it. Whether positively or negatively, however they view it, fear is there for most people. But not at Summerhill. There are certain things that cause me to be anxious, but I sort of rationalise myself through it. Maybe the difference between Summerhill and elsewhere is that at Summerhill there was no reason to be fearful, but other people do have real reason to be fearful. The system relies on their fear. I think that for other people their interactions with their fellow humans is a more fearful business than it is for me, and is driven by fear in more ways than it is for me.

I think I would make the analogy that if you're a blind person, no matter how well you know that roadway, or that corridor, you will probably mostly have your hands out. Whereas I would say that I can see that road and I can see that corridor. And I can see the effects that my interaction with other people has. Reading signals off them. They're a language to me. I'm not blind in that circumstance. Maybe I'm just the simpleton in this; in fact I'm walking along my road thinking I can see and – whop! I've hit the bloody lamppost that I couldn't see. But what it feels like for me is that other people are afraid of what others may think of them. Whereas I will know what they think of me. I actually will know it. I know what it is. I'm not imagining it. You know, if they're angry with me or if they despise me, I know it. And so I'm not wrestling with my own demons, interpreting or second-guessing what people are actually thinking. I think I've learnt to read the signs.

At Summerhill everything was out on the table. The cards were on the table all the time. You live being part of a very small community and you're surrounded by these people for twelve weeks at a shot. There's no going away from them. You get to know them terribly well. And so if you use these as models for what the rest of humankind might be like, you've got a bloody accurate picture. Most people don't have that chance. At best they will engage with those kinds of relationships within their own family, and even then that's quite often not the case because of the conflicts within the family. The emotional ties that we have with each other, within families, are very strong and somehow blinding to many other things. I mean, I can remember saying to my mum, "Oh, don't tell me what you think about so-and-so because as soon as you've said it I can't think my own thought." But as a child, when you're dealing with peers, you don't have that; you don't have somebody's powerful vision turning everything towards or away from your own vision.

The General Meeting is the crucial thing in all this. I describe it as being the public element of self. There's a private element of self, part of which chooses whether to go to lessons or not, and you understand and suffer the consequences of your decisions on a personal level. The meeting is the public self where you understand the implications of any decision you make on a public level. If I voted for us all to stay up late, and that's what happened, maybe people would be overtired, or maybe it would be great fun because it's the end of term, or whatever – but you actually do get the chance to see what you do and how it affects other people. It's an information network as well. If you miss a meeting, you miss out on what's happening. You don't know what's going to come up next week. So kids tip up for that reason as much as they turn up to bring anybody up. And it's also a social thing. It's interesting to hear what other people think about stuff. And even if you don't join in, you're learning how the community feels about x, y and z. You know, if I'm going to do this dastardly deed what's likely to happen? I was always a fairly animated speaker at meetings. I find that stuff fascinating.

At Summerhill the journey you're taking is a journey of self-discovery. You come to know yourself. And Summerhill today looks the same as it's always looked; though the children are different and the outside world is different. Summerhill is so much the same that I could go back and live there again and I'd know what to do. I'd know how to be. The question it raises is, is it just a very subtle form of indoctrination? The fact that it promotes things like human growth, happiness – those qualities that some people believe are valuable – doesn't make it any less a form of indoctrination than anything else. But I take a moral view, and my moral view is that I shall not willingly do anyone any harm. And I want to live in a community where the people I live with will take the same view, because I want to be part of a cherished and cherishing group – to put it in a raw, simple way. But, having said all that, I have made a very distinct stand. I mean I take notions of 'good' and 'cherish', and I write them up and say they're cuddly, lovely words and I'm happy to live with them. Somebody else might give me another view that says all that does is distort your view of pain. And so it goes on.

I do feel despair. Massively. Much of the time. About the various positions one finds oneself in that you can do nothing about. Both internally and externally. You look at things that are happening in the world and you know there is nothing you can do about them. And in my work I've always been fantastically frustrated by the kind of people one has to work with. People who have the power and no imagination. Or the kind of people that find people like me very threatening and cause us to remain outside, marginalised. But then, on the other hand, I look at myself and I say, if this has happened consistently it must be something I'm doing. And, you know, that's a dilemma.

I don't actually ponder the meaning of life. I don't mind that there's no meaning. It's an irrelevance. I consider myself part of these social animals we are that are human beings. I don't have a sense of worth in that we're here for any purpose, or there's something of us when we're gone. I don't mind one way or the other. It doesn't motivate me; it doesn't stop me doing anything.

One difference with Summerhill today is that it's operating in a society where it's under much greater pressure to conform than it ever was when Neill was alive, because by the time Neill was becoming famous he'd already been doing this for 40-odd years; and he was part of a huge cultural movement that approved of him, not simply one or two people saying, Oh, that's nice. So Zoë's in the position of defending Summerhill, which he didn't really have to do. He just broadcast. But Summerhill actually not only could offer mainstream education a lesson, it can also offer fantastic insights into what kids are like and what their potential is. Unfortunately it hasn't thus far taken the bull by the horns and said, Right, we've been doing it for 70-odd years, perhaps you might like to come and share the experience with us?

Summerhill doesn't sell itself. Lots of people visit. It's always had loads of visitors, but it doesn't have a sense of what it knows that they don't know. Because it doesn't know them it can't sell itself. It's a bit like, if all I've ever seen of you is from above the waist, and actually I'm a cobbler – because I haven't looked over the fence and seen that you've got feet too, I've never thought to say to you, Hey, I make shoes, I'll make you some shoes.

So it suffers from insularity and lack of confidence. It sees itself in a defensive role. But if you have utter conviction in what you do, and that everyone else is doing the wrong thing, then you could step out and say, It's not really like that. This is what I try to do in my work, whenever I get the chance. Not directly. I don't say, Summerhill, blah, blah... But what I am able to say is, People, blah, blah... Things are fine as long as they work to the mutual satisfaction of all. But if somebody's actually doing it for their own glory, or their own benefit at the expense of other people, then it must be wrong. It's as simple as that. But of course our culture is, when somebody says, Jump, you just say,

How high?

That's the result of conditioning. That's what schooling is. Education in the mainstream is about learning how to be wrong. No child before school knows about being wrong. They know things that don't work and won't go their way. They don't know that they're wrong. They learn that. That's what they learn when they go to school. What kids need is to operate with other children. If all the adults disappeared the kids at Summerhill could carry on. Whereas if the adults pulled out of a comprehensive school all hell would break out. Adults are not important. I only noticed how 'important' adults were when I left Summerhill. Perhaps because they were never valued themselves as kids. It's power. But if you'd just let go of power, you'd find that the whole of society actually wouldn't topple down.

Postscript (2011)

Since this interview was done in the mid 1990s, I have moved employment three times. First to the Royal College of Surgeons of England, where I was Curriculum Project Manager for the Joint Committee on Higher Surgical Training, then to City University London, where I was interprofessional education lead for City and Queen Mary, and now I am a Senior Lecturer in Medical Education at Barts and The London School of Medicine and Dentistry, Queen Mary University of London.

My current role continues to encompass interprofessional education – for the healthcare students of both City University and QM – but also includes faculty development relating primarily to teacher education for medics, and curriculum development and scholarship in undergraduate and postgraduate medical education.

In terms of my opinions about things: I don't think that any of my deep ideas, beliefs or values have changed with the passing of time – I think that they have just refined with the experiences that I have gained through living my life.

Lucien Crofts
1970-77

The resourcefulness and flexibility of those who do not opt for, or are not suited to, traditional career paths, is one of the most encouraging outcomes of Summerhill education. Unlike many people who feel themselves all at sea upon leaving school with few or no academic qualifications, Lucien Crofts acquired a number of useful skills, both during his time at Summerhill and after, which have resulted in him branching out in various interesting directions.

Lucien Crofts's parents split up when he was about 15 months old and he spent the first part of his life living with his grandparents – "So that first important early stage I was brought up by a wartime generation, which is sort of interesting." The grandparents' home was in Cornwall, on the edge of Bodmin Moor. Lucien remembers it as being a bit lonely – "especially if you're an only child with grandparents, but a seriously nice playground as well."

Although obviously confused by what had happened, he also felt fairly happy and settled. "My grandparents, having retired, did a better job of being parents than they had with their own kids. I got more or less undivided attention from them. They had nothing much else to do but be good to me. I think my granddad found something of himself again. He learnt to play. There's always guilt attached to these things and I think he was trying to be a brother and a father, and God knows what else, and he did a bloody good job considering he was in his late sixties."

Lucien's mother had been trying to cope with him and his younger brother, and had not succeeded. "She was falling to pieces pretty much. Social Services stepped in – and my grandparents saved the situation as far as I was concerned." His brother was less fortunate and was put up for adoption because the grandparents couldn't take both of them. This is understandably a matter of regret for Lucien. "They tend not to split siblings up nowadays, but then – so I've got a brother somewhere who is my only true blood sibling, and I was made an only child when I wasn't."

Lucien didn't see much of either of his parents for a long time, though he remembers a court battle for custody when he was about two-and-a-half. "Someone asked me, 'What would you like to do?' And apparently I broke down in tears and said, 'I want to go back to my grandparents.'"

He did and stayed with them for another two years. Then one day his father turned up in a sports car with another woman and took him away. This time his father secured custody, though fortunately for Lucien he maintained close contact with his grandparents. "My granddad was my dad emotionally, so I feel that I was orphaned when he died. I was emotionally distanced from my real dad. That's in the past and I now have a good relationship with him; but at the time I basically had other ideas as to who my parents were – they were much older."

Lucien's father made the decision to send him to Summerhill, later telling him he had sent him there to save him from himself. Before that Lucien had attended a couple of conventional primary schools. His grandparents helped with the Summerhill fees – "though being old school they were much more unsure about the lack of discipline and so on." When Lucien stayed with them in the holidays he remembers them being a bit worried about his lack of progress in reading and writing. "They used to hassle me about that, which probably kept me not doing things at school for longer."

During his first two years at Summerhill Lucien remembers being chronically homesick and insecure. This may have been in part due to a badly handled introduction. Both his parents took him there and both neglected to say goodbye. "I'd started talking to my housemother and playing with one of the kids and I turned round – and they were gone." This abrupt separation affected Lucien badly for some time. "It leaves a very lasting impression, because there were these people I'd just started to get used to – and they were gone. They'd done the same thing as they had when I was younger." Once again he had been abandoned, alone in a strange place. "I was absolutely miserable as sin, phoning them up every night in tears. I couldn't get out of this awful place."

There were other instances of parental ineptitude that Lucien remembers, one of them occurring when he returned late to school, a few days after term started. "My dad put me on the train to Saxmundham and said, 'I'll make sure Ena picks you up.' But he didn't bother to phone her." Lucien was left alone on the station, waiting for the lift that never came, becoming more and more upset. Eventually he phoned the school. "Ena said, 'What's the problem, why don't you just come and find us?' But the thing is I was riddled with insecurity. My dad kept doing stuff like that to me. Nowadays he wouldn't do that. I think he's learnt from his mistakes and become a much better parent to his subsequent children."

It was some time before Lucien began to feel secure at Summerhill. "I basically spent the first couple of years just fucking terrified most of the time. There were two or three, I suppose, problem kids, and they tested me. Two of them later became my best friends." It took Lucien some time to figure out how Summerhill worked and the central function of the General Meeting. "I didn't understand about bringing people up. I didn't really know or trust anyone. I was still in the 'go to adults' mode about all those things."

It was also difficult for him making the transition from being a child who was the focus of attention of indulgent grandparents to being one of 10 children looked after by a single housemother. "I think some of the more straight-ahead, down-to-earth, roughnecked Summerhill kids looked on me as a bit of a tart. I had my first ever fight at Summerhill. I think a lot of these kids had problem parents, as Neill called them. A lot of us were like that."

Neill was still alive for the first two or three years of Lucien's time at Summerhill, and he vaguely remembers having some PLs with him. "I think he probably did do some good, but you kind of wouldn't know, especially with Neill's way of doing therapy. The kid didn't realise it was happening. You can't say, 'You are going to therapy.' Well, Americans might do." In the latter part of his life Neill was gradually winding down the practice of giving PLs. "He'd come to the conclusion that whether kids had them or not they seemed to sort themselves out through the freedom thing."

Lucien liked Neill because he reminded him a little bit of his grandfather – "wandering about always with kids hanging around him, dressed in baggy corduroy trousers and a well-worn jacket. He was the sort who always had string, sealing wax and a penknife in his pocket. So that was quite nice. But I didn't have a very close relationship with him.*"

Ena was very far from being the benevolent old person that Neill had been. As Lucien says, "Everyone was shit scared of Ena. She was pretty hard when we were kids there." Later, he was to revise his opinion. "I saw a side of her, and her fears and frailties, that she never showed when she was staff. I think she found running Summerhill pretty scary. It was such a huge responsibility and a hell of an act to follow. She had a tough, hard exterior, and I don't think it was that bad for Summerhill. She has her place there, and that's how some practical people express those things. I'm not sure that she lacked the intuitive bit. Basically she was pretty bloody honest. If she was pissed off she let you know it, but she never held any grudges."

Lucien had to struggle with learning difficulties, possibly made worse by his experience at his previous schools. "I don't know whether I had dyslexia, but I had problems with writing, and when I'm tired I still have a problem with it. I was always terrified, because in my old schools there was the teacher standing over me, and I'd just freeze and block. That's always been with me, so maybe that's why I went into business for myself."

Some of the teachers at Summerhill were aware of Lucien's problems, in particular Peter Woods. "I was very close to Peter. It may sound funny, but I seriously loved the guy. I did an awful lot of pottery with him. I suppose I adopted him as a bit of a father figure. He was a very brilliant guy; brilliant potter. He'd studied under Bernard Leach; studied all the Japanese stuff. One holiday I didn't go home; I stayed at Summerhill just to study with him. I became pretty good at

---

* Neill died on 22nd September, 1973 in Aldeburgh Cottage Hospital, just 25 days short of his 90th birthday. A few days' later the pupils returned to Summerhill for the start of the new term, with Ena in charge.

pottery myself, but I suppose my relationship with him went down a bit towards the end and I started to give up on it. It just sort of died on me anyway. I never touched pottery for 15 years after I left Summerhill. I couldn't do it. About a year after I left I received a postcard saying, 'Unfortunately Peter Woods died.' I went down for the funeral, but the train was late, so I missed it."

Apart from pottery, Lucien was interested in ecology and science – "albeit making gunpowder and bombs and stuff. I loved all that. The science teacher was a bit of a kid – 'Let's go and let this rocket off.' Then, if you wanted to know what the chemicals did, he'd tell you. Whether he was a good teacher or not, who knows? I got very close to the ecology teacher, Maggie. Of all the teachers she was the best. I learnt a lot about ecology." Like other Summerhillians, Lucien is of the opinion that some of the staff were problem people themselves, and variable in their teaching abilities. "Some were brilliant and some weren't."

Lucien can only remember chairing a meeting twice. "Towards the end of my time I got quite reclusive. I seem to remember a year I did nothing but read. I read *Lord of the Rings* four times, and anything interesting I could find in the library, which was not easy I have to say. I hear it's improved now. God, it was crap. I suppose I read so much because I'd come to reading late. I learnt to read by myself, by doing it. And I taught myself to write. I don't remember asking any teachers to help because I just didn't want to know. So Neill's theory about leaving kids alone and they'll come to it in their own time worked in my case."

The reluctance to attend formal lessons continued. "Ena did say in my last year, 'Look, don't you think you ought to start doing some lessons? You haven't got very long.' Which was kind of unheard of in Summerhill. It was out of concern, but…I had a flurry of going to lessons and then towards the end I stopped. I never went as far as 'O' levels."

Lucien recollects being depressed about the prospect of leaving. It was the continuance of the pattern established early in his life. "Another impending loss of people I cared about."

After Summerhill

Fortunately, Summerhill had sorted out enough of my learning problems to make me want to go to lessons again – and then it was time to leave. I think a long time back, maybe before the war, Summerhill used to keep kids till 18. I really wished they did that. I wish I'd had another couple of years there. I'd had my recluse stage, and I was beginning to feel I wanted to get back into school life again. Start getting involved in the community as an older kid. People work at different speeds. It was my home – it had started to work for me and then I was out. I don't adjust to change quickly. I find it quite stressful. But once I've really locked into something, then I'm there, and it's just as hard for me to readjust back out of it again.

I used to have this recurring dream where I went back to Summerhill as an adult, and got another chance. I went back and had my room in the Carriages, and got to do it again – the bits I didn't do then. I always woke up feeling like I'd just left, and feeling quite out of sorts and sad.

Unlike a lot of Summerhillians who went on to college, I went to work. My first job happened by accident and it led me into what I'm doing now, which is music technology, and it was the best possible start I could have had. It was absolutely at the cutting edge of using this kind of technology. It's interesting that all this stuff is actually going on, not in London, but in the country, around Oxfordshire and places like that. There's some of the brightest sparks in the world lurking round these country lanes. Solid state logic started in a little 16-track studio in Oxfordshire with a couple of guys who designed and built their own mixing consul, and I was just fortunate to be there at the time.

I was 17/18 and just dossing around my dad's pub, and Colin Bateman, who was the engineer, used to come in for a beer, and I got to know him. He thought Summerhill was quite a natty idea, and he knew I was into hi-fi, so he said, "Why don't you come up and I'll pay you thirty pounds to be assistant engineer and learn a bit about studios and untangle people's guitar leads and roll their joints for them?" So I did. This was when the 16-track was big. Colin Sanders, who was the boss and an incredibly talented designer and engineer himself, didn't like or think any of the stuff on the market was any bloody good. So he designed his own desk for his studio, and some of the producers who came in with the bands, including Greg Lake who was producing a band called Spitfire, said, "This desk is absolutely the fucking bollocks. You ought to exhibit that at one of the APRS shows in London." "Nah, get away." But he convinced him, and he did in the end. He sold three on the stand and never looked back. And ended up making the best desks in the world. The Beeb have got eight or 10 of them. Now everybody's got one.

Colin Sanders was an inspiration to me. The way he works. He's not a musician, but he loves music and he's into technology and the absolute quality of production. I can be a bit of a perfectionist. I've had to back off certain things I really used to chew to death. But you mostly have to stop at some point – it's good enough – and go back to it later. I now don't have a problem with that, but I used to.

It was my first job and probably the only job I've worked in where there was a genuine total motivation through pride and interest in all the stuff. It was designed by musicians and engineers for musicians and engineers, which is why it was so good. Everyone was into it in one form or another, and some of the world's most famous people would come by. Peter Gabriel would turn up and wander round and chat to people, and you'd walk into reception and there'd be Pete Townshend chatting to the secretary. "Oh, hi, Peter." And not, "Oh, I've just met Pete Townshend." It was normal. I didn't feel there was a wow to it. I've had a chat to Kate Bush and so what? Those were our standard clients, and that was my first taste of work.

So all this happened, and I was there by chance. I was there for seven years, just being around the right place at the right time. It was bloody hard too. Learning to relate to people without that Summerhill understanding and the Meeting to support you was a shock; and I didn't cope very well to start with. I had to learn some pretty hard lessons pretty quickly, because I got my fingers badly burned. For example, boy and girl relationships at Summerhill were pretty easy and we didn't have people nicking other people's girlfriends, which are basic things. You go out into the real world and you realise she's just split up with her boyfriend, and what she's trying to do is use you to make him jealous to see if he'll take her back. Men and women used each other. I found that quite frustrating. I was quite naïve. That kind of thing didn't really happen at Summerhill.

Of course, everyone plays games, and there were some going on at Summerhill, but it was still a bit different really. We all do it, and we have to learn to do it – in business and relationships – a bit. But deep down you really despise that kind of behaviour. That is the bit about the world outside, and what I have to become to deal with it, that I don't like. The world is a very different place outside Summerhill. Summerhill prepares you well in certain things, but it actually de-prepares you for a lot of it. You don't have that amount of caring attitude out here. You don't have a working, high-speed, real-type democracy. It's all too big. And it's not full of Summerhillians anyway. There are certain areas in which you mature more genuinely through Summerhill, which may not happen so readily with people going through conventional things. Equally, in other areas it makes you incredibly naïve, whereas the rest of the world is not naïve in those areas (though it may be undernourished in the sense that Summerhill nourishes you). And the areas where the world's expecting you to be fairly hardened are the areas where Summerhill's pretty naïve.

There are issues you have to deal with that are not easy, especially when you go into business for yourself. I ran my own business, with a partner, for a while, making electronics. We were subcontracting manufacturers. We were making things for the military and had to sign the Official Secrets Act. Some of my gismos may have ended up in things that kill people, and I had to be willing to shelve my conscience and do the job. I didn't feel all that comfortable about it, but there's a side that needs to be debated – are you willing to do something which will kill someone you've never met? Are you willing to have a vague link to something that's killed a stranger? But these things are actually necessary. I've said that to some Summerhillians and they're absolutely appalled. You get the right-on responses – why would you want to do something like that? But it isn't that simple. I said to one of them, "Look, you're a guitarist, you've got your band. If I came to one of your gigs and said, 'You're brilliant, I'll sign you but I don't want the rest of the guys,' I know bloody well you'd jump and leave your mates behind if you had to." He said, "Of course." I said, "Well, okay, basically it's doing what you have to do to get where you want to." Who is to say, well that is necessary in the real world to get on? There are all sorts of issues like this. In actual fact I did the contract as soon as I could and then withdrew.

It's easy when you're at Summerhill to have these big pure pacifist ideas. And a lot of them are dyed-in-the-wool socialists, or like to think they are. Politically they all climb into that. Yes, Summerhill has got some fundamental socialism there, but at the same time it's teeming with free enterprise, and everybody's got the biggest possible ego to go with it too. But it seems everyone has two or three of these little political sweeties they take into the world, and I actually don't think they're being very realistic. They're a little bit sort of right-on. And I find that a bit corny actually.

Some people say I went into business because I'm not a creative person, but business is highly creative. The vision – that's where business is interesting; that is where it's highly creative – deciding your route. It's just so much fun; it's a mega buzz. It's only a little bit short – once you get really cooking on something like that – it's not far short of the buzz you get after having performed, coming off stage. Being creative, whether it's art or anything else, is basically creative thinking. It applies to the medium and it comes from within. There is a bit of artist's snobbery about business. But, you think you're being creative, you bloody see what it takes to do that – to run a business – to do it really well. It'll keep you absolutely on your toes – in terms of challenges and time. You've got to get shit hot at getting round those things, and taking advantage of developing new things, new customers. We were the third largest electronic subcontractor in the land, turning over a million a year. But my partner kind of got cold feet over a lot of it and decided to play it safe. We started going in different directions and I became unhappy, disillusioned, and walked away. Now I've come full circle and I'm back where I started, with music technology, which I'm very happy with.

What I've learned from running my own business is that whatever you do is made real – shit or bust. You can't hide behind slogans. And it works best as a team effort, though a lot of people don't treat it like that. I adopted some of Colin Sanders's attitudes towards the way I treated staff. I made them more self-motivated. I was also drawing on Summerhill as a community that works and sorts things out pretty efficiently. You could apply some of those fundamental Summerhill attitudes to business without having these designer ideas. Shareholding schemes, true co-operatives, would be there automatically. What a great way to start exploring. Yes, you still have to be hard-nosed and not take any shit, but there's a more positive structure within that. And Summerhill should be trying to interface more with the real world – bringing business studies onto the curriculum would help. Kids starting proper businesses. What a great way of making some of the Summerhill things live in the real world. It's going to teach an awful lot of non-Summerhill people about working, and also provide a better bridge for the kids when they go out there, which the school doesn't do very well at present. There is a bit of an island mentality to the place, because it is under siege a lot of the time. But like every secure castle, however many enemy there are outside knocking on the door, every castle becomes the besieged prisoner's cell.

I've found that a lot of Summerhillians have been almost tainted by the real world. I don't know whether that's a conscious or unconscious thing, but they've changed. I don't think they look back very much now. I don't think they compare. I do. I still see Summerhill with those references. I'm always aware when I'm having to play a game, or spot someone else doing it, thinking, "God, this is such a pile of shit. I really don't want to have to do this." Okay, I will, but it's always kind of begrudging somehow. But some of my closest friends from Summerhill, I actually can't relate to them any more.

They've gone very much into the materialistic, hard-edged world. The London thing in particular doesn't suit me. I'm really sick of some of the games people play.

The people I see now generally have more disillusioned things to say about Summerhill. Underneath you can hear it coming through. They're disillusioned or pissed off. Some say Summerhill didn't push kids enough academically. Summerhill should have done more. Summerhill failed them. I think there are some who resent or blame whatever they perceive as their own failure on Summerhill. The whole thing about Summerhill is – "I'm willing to take responsibility for myself. I don't have to go to lessons; I have the choice to do so. If I don't go, I've made the choice. It is not anyone else's fault." The facilities were there. That is the nature of the beast. A lot of people blame something outside themselves. When you hear Summerhillians do that, you think, "Christ, I feel they've fundamentally missed the point about the whole thing." That is the fundamental Summerhill thing – the freedom to do. It's not the freedom not to do. And try to learn to be positive when you're doing it.

There's a part of me that says I would rather remain sensitised and a bit naïve, and actually get turfed over sometimes, than become hard-bitten and – callous isn't the right word. They've all become rather disturbingly cynical. They may play games better, they may not get turfed over so often, they may be more successful and whatever, but I do feel they're selling out. I don't like that in people. There's only so much of that I will do to survive. I'd rather take a fall. I still have this innocent-until-proven-guilty attitude. Of course you're going to come a cropper sometimes, but if you get cynical it's like mistrust first, then earn my respect. Prove me wrong. I've seen that in some Summerhillians. What is cynicism but one person protecting themselves from other cynics? I think that's sad. I think that is wrong.

I deliberately stayed away from Summerhill for a long time; then, having done this nothing-to-do-with-Summerhill, real world thing, I thought when I came to London I'd have a top-up of less cynicism, and actually found the Summerhillians here were the same as everyone else now. There are common references, but I'm pretty disillusioned.

The two things it seems my generation of Summerhillians don't do is a) get married and b) go to church. The majority of them – the ones I've met – on principle just think it's a pile of crap for some reason. They can't seem to accept the one or two Summerhillians who have done differently. I say, "No, Summerhillians, you do what you feel is right for you." There's almost an inverted snobbery attached to it – "We are Summerhillians, we know better than Christ and we know better than this." In fact all they're doing is exactly the same as the people they're complaining about, if the truth be known. I've seen an awful lot of that, and it's bollocks. You have to learn from both parties and, with or without the Summerhill thing, you're still basically just talking about people. And in fact Summerhillians are no different. And it shows because they're just as capable of being snobbish. With some of the more right-on and gay issues it tends to show and be focused on things like that. You're wrong to be abusive to a gay person and hassle them, but it's okay for gays to out people. It's okay because being gay and right-on is a freedom thing. It's all right being disrespectful and destructive if it's in the name of being gay. And you think, bollocks. All these people are just as capable of being prejudiced and suspicious and jealous.

I'm not slagging Summerhill off, but Summerhill is actually what you do with it and how you handle it. And I wonder about how well some people handle it, particularly Summerhillians who still socialise and stick together. They're hardened by the real world, but at the same time they've never really left Summerhill either. They don't really talk at Summerhill about really deep sort of emotional things – they just have these opinions about everything. We're known for being opinionated, because we're able to express ourselves. But it's still the quality of your opinions that counts, not whether you've got them or not. At Summerhill the fundamental thing to me was that you could understand someone else's point of view and respect it and still fundamentally disagree with it. You respected differences. That's the key to the whole thing. I seem to find that Summerhillians, of whatever generations, are stuck with this thing of being more right, but not actually showing any understanding of something different to them. It's about time they learnt that trick. If you fundamentally disagree with something, fine, you can agree to differ. It's almost, if necessary, respecting your enemy. But there's this attitude of, "Well, we're right." And I think that makes a person more blind than the one who's prepared to say, "I don't agree with Summerhill." They must have listened to you to some degree to make that opinion. Summerhillians have just decided certain things are wrong and that's it. They're stuck with these attitudes. It may be more common in London because it's a protection mechanism and London is a more hard-edged place. You kind of need sandbags. I didn't want to do that. It's funny, because I'm still on good terms with the people here that are nothing to do with Summerhill. The people I've just met from scratch. Got no problem with those, anti-Summerhill warts and all. Just accept them for who they are.

Most people would say I'm not into the Summmerhill thing, but I'd argue I'm closer to Summerhill than they are now. Instead of going back there I'm trying to use some of the things that are fundamental to it. It feels like a spiritual thing. There's only so much I can say intellectually about it. It's all been said before. It's a fundamental belief that never goes. It's not a religion, but it's like one way of making love – hope and humanity. The nicest side of humanity – that was made real there.

If I don't feel comfortable about going back there because of who's there, or feeling how small everything looks now compared to when I was there, then I don't go. It really is something you have to leave behind. Like leaving your childhood behind and then applying what you are left with internally to real life. This latent uncomfortableness – it'll pass. Not all bad, not all good, but I don't have any major gripes about Summerhill. Not the fundamentals of what was going on. Summerhill's always about you never stop growing and learning. What it did was put me off conventional schooling, but it sure as hell left me with a childlike thirst for knowledge. Ordinary school had beaten that out of me. I think that's the argument – it's good if you get some formal qualifications from Summerhill, but in fact, if you haven't, it doesn't matter anyway. One way or the other, whether you've got a bit of paper or not, you've got to get in there and demonstrate you can do the job. Because employers don't give a shit about anything else. That's the thing that matters. And yes, it's true. It's there and it works.

I've obviously spent a lot of my time – and married one – with people who went through the standard school system. They told me about their schooldays, the emotional blackmail and the games and being put under pressure, the whole thing. I feel I do not want my kids subjected to that. It wouldn't be simply that I think my kids should have the choice over whether to go to lessons. It's more to do with developing a deeper understanding about some of those things I've mentioned. It's not that I wouldn't trust my kids. I wouldn't want them to be in any other place. But if they did go to Summerhill, I would hope that they'd have contact with the bigger world. I was totally lost in Summerhill, so it was a much bigger shock when I left.

Postscript (2005)

Since doing this interview I've worked again for a time in music technology as a freelance. Then for a couple of years I worked as a thatcher's mate using the traditional methods. We grew our own thatch and did the harvest. I drove an eighty-year-old binder. It was a fascinating job, learning the old methods. I worked harder than on any other job I've ever done. It was also well-paid. Then I ran a village 'telecottage', providing fax, internet and photocopying etc. for a rural community, long before internet cafés came on the scene.

After that I went back to working in pubs. Now I'm the landlord of a pub in Bristol, where my father used to run a pub, so in a sense I've come full circle. I married again and my wife and I are joint leaseholders. We've got two kids and another on the way. Both of us would be happy for them all to go to Summerhill, if we can afford it. My wife hated her school.

The book that most inspires me is *The Prophet* by Kahlil Gibrain. It fits in well with the philosophy of Summerhill. Core Christianity is also fine – I have no problem with that. It's about the quality of life, and not fearing death. Neill was trying to let the good in people come forth, with absence of fear. It's about the democracy of emotions – don't let fear have the casting vote. Acknowledge it, but don't submit to it. I can tie Neill in with Gilbrain and Jesus Christ and Ghandi – they all have similar beliefs. We have to give room for spirituality. Fear kills love, not death.

(2011)

I ran a couple of pubs for four years and then did property maintenance for a community housing association with which I was connected. I still live in Bristol and now have four children who I hope to send to Summerhill, when I can afford it. I've played bass guitar in various bands over the years – mainly heavy rock and blues. I'm now training to be a psychotherapist.

Clare Harvie
1973-78

The experience of Clare Harvie, who left Summerhill early to attend another, more conventional and academically-oriented boarding school, and later became a teacher herself in racially and culturally mixed inner-city London schools, raises the question of the extent to which Summerhill values and practices can, or should, be translated into settings where a quite different set of assumptions and problems obtain. It also illustrates the significant difference between Summerhill and the vast majority of other educational institutions.

Clare Harvie's mother, Janet, was born into a Calvinist middle-class family living in the small village of Dunlop in Ayrshire, in the West of Scotland. Clare has retained her mother's family name. After working some years for the Royal Overseas League, Janet Harvie took a post in Sierra Leone, West Africa. While there she met Clare's father who came from a highly-educated Creole family. At the turn of the 19th/20th centuries, his ancestors were the first black Africans to read law at Durham University. Her mother came home to England to have Clare and never returned to Sierra Leone.

It was Janet Harvie's break with convention that led her to take a post as houseparent at Summerhill, and take her daughter with her. "Although I was happy at primary school in Torquay, my mother thought that Summerhill would be beneficial for me. She hoped that I would flourish and thrive in the progressive environment. So it wasn't because I had any problems as such that my mother decided I should go to Summerhill, which I think was the case with some people there."

So mother and daughter started at Summerhill together. "It didn't make it any easier going with my mother. In fact it made it more difficult. But we didn't live together. My mother was in Cottage with younger children and I was in House." Clare's first impressions were not favourable. "The children seemed quite rude. They would say things and comment on your colour in a very uninhibited way. I remember a boy on a bike, about my own age, shouting things at me about my colour. I'm not saying racial abuse was a big thing, but that was one of the things I remember from the first day or week. It sticks in my mind."

There was one black person at Summerhill whom Clare remembers, an American girl about a year younger. There were a lot of Americans, French and Belgians. Clare enjoyed the communal living. "Being in House was really good fun. Having been an only child, I was now sharing a room with lots of other children, staying up late, having midnight feasts and all that. The downside of course was when you were ill." There was actually no place to be ill, the sanatorium having been taken over for accommodation shortly after it was built. "So if you had flu or something, you'd just be in bed in the same room with all the fun still going on around you." Clare also had the feeling that nothing was safe. "Although people had their own tuck-boxes, they would get broken into. I think it was mainly to get food. I seem to remember this obsession with getting chocolate and biscuits, not so much your personal possessions, although that was probably happening as well. There were quite a lot of problem kids there at that time."

The American influence was very strong. "It was in the language and the way people looked. Some of them came from quite big families and they seemed very loud and confident." Clare remembers a very hippy feel in the first year and it was, generally speaking, an enjoyable atmosphere. "There was quite a pool of older pupils who'd been there a very long time and I think that gave the feeling of the place being a happy place to be. It didn't feel stagnant." However, Clare's opinion was to change. "Towards the time I was leaving it felt there were better things going on elsewhere. I don't know whether that's just the age. You want more."

The fact that pupils didn't have to go to lessons didn't really register at first. "It was more the new way of living, and the distinct lack of privacy combined with the sheer enjoyment of having so many people around. So, it does sound silly, but I wasn't immediately aware of there not being compulsory lessons. I'm talking about the first term.

We didn't have very structured classes. I don't remember really sitting down. We seemed to do a lot of sewing and making things. Some children were still learning English, which may have been a bit of a problem."

Clare continued to see quite a lot of her mother. "But I didn't spend a lot of time with her on my own. I think she was very popular and obviously at that age some children will get quite attached to a member of staff. But even though you're an only child, you get used to that." She gradually lost touch with her friends in Torquay. "You become more dependent on your school friends – they come to stay with you in the holidays, or you go to stay with them. So your life becomes more Summerhill-centred."

People were always making things at Summerhill and crazes would come and go. "Crazes for making a particular type of bike, for example. It doesn't sound very pc now, but girls didn't seem to be making bikes. I remember the girls had a craze for making rag dolls and people spent a lot of time in the woodwork shop. There was real enthusiasm for making things in general. That sticks in my mind. I'm not sure if people were exceptionally creative or they were being creative because that was one of the main outlets for channelling your energy. The woodwork shed and the art room were nice, comfortable places, enjoyable places to be. Making dresses for the end-of-term parties was another popular activity. So far as I remember, biology was the most well attended of the more academic classes – English and maths far less so. And the mathematics class was mainly boys, I think."

Clare was keen to dispel the myth that a particular type of person sends their child to Summerhill. "I get the impression that a lot of people think that because parents sent their children to Summerhill, the parents were very left-wing or had very liberal or progressive views. That is definitely not the case. They were sent there for a variety of reasons. Maybe they were very disturbed; maybe it was just the last hope. Perhaps parents were hoping it was going to make them exceptional." In common with other Summerhillians, Clare remembers that many of the problem kids did improve. "One in particular was very disturbed. I was absolutely terrified of him. A lot of people were. He was a very frightening child, but he turned out okay." On the other hand there were those who did not improve. "I think Summerhill probably made it worse for some. There comes a point where their energy needs to be channelled. They've broken out and they think, Where do I go from here? For some children it was a problem, both socially and academically."

General Meetings and Tribunals were basically effective in Clare's opinion. She was herself the subject of a special meeting. "It was a joke that went wrong, involving myself and two other girls. They didn't really know who it was, who was responsible. But it was resolved. The general disgust that everyone showed was in itself a punishment. So Tribunals do work, yes."

Neill was still alive when Clare first went to Summerhill. "I remember him asking me to move the guinea fowl out of the way. I think that was my first encounter. Initially when I spoke to him I was a bit frightened because I was expecting a headmaster. I had an idea of what a headmaster was and he wasn't like that. But I didn't have any PLs [Private Lessons] or much to do with him and he died in my first year."

The adult Clare remembers most from Summerhill is Peter Wood. "I did pottery with him and he was an outstanding potter, but more than that he was a really nice person – just his heart, this whole little air that he had about him was a nice place to be. And I think that through him you had access to the outside world. He had all these *Time* magazines and you felt that by seeing him you were getting to know a little of what life was like outside. There were a lot of interesting things to talk about and read. He was a person I'd go back and visit. He is one of the main people in my memory of Summerhill. A very big person in my life there. I was sad when he died."

After Summerhill

I left Summerhill early because in my last year there I wasn't really very happy. I'd been in a situation with quite serious bullying. I felt also that it was getting quite boring by that stage – there didn't seem to be enough going on. Perhaps it was my age. I wanted the opportunity to meet more people, to live in a wider circle. My mother had left by then to work in another school and I went to a comprehensive in Devon that had boarders as well. I was quite nervous about going there and it turned out to be quite a shock. The regime seemed really barbaric. But I enjoyed meeting other children and I made lots of friends there.

The fact that it was stricter than Summerhill didn't matter so much during the day because you had a timetable, but in the evening silly little things like how you decorated your room seemed really impossible. You weren't allowed to put posters on your wall, for example; and once I wrote happy birthday to somebody in my text book, which in Summerhill wouldn't be a big deal. But you got really told off for doing things like that, so it was a bit trivial. I didn't really like having set work, which is something I wasn't used to. Summerhill is all about working on your own. As a teenager you decided vaguely when you went to bed, what time you got up. Your time was your own. So in some areas it was really unpleasant at this new school. But on the other hand, having a structured timetable was quite nice. I enjoyed the classes, but they wanted me to take 12 'O' levels, which seemed a lot. I asked if I could limit it to five, but they had this theory that it was best for people to take as many exams as they could, which seemed a bit silly really. Quite unnecessary.

So far as relating to the teachers, it was very much 'Sir' or 'Miss'. No first names. Generally speaking I found the teaching good, but obviously you only saw the professional side of the teachers, whereas in Summerhill you got to know them as people. But I got on with the teachers all right. There wasn't what you'd call a discipline problem. They all found I was very conscientious and, generally speaking, if there was a problem it would probably be in the restrictions of the actual boarding.

I got some 'O' levels and went into the Lower VIth and started 'A' levels – but then I decided to go to London. I wanted to study but I didn't want to stay in school. I wanted to go to a sixth-form college. I had never lived in London and I thought it would be a really amazing place to see. I don't know about that now, but it seemed like a really good idea. I went first to live in Hylda Sims's house – I'd known her daughter at Summerhill – and went to Southwark College, which is an inner-city college. I liked the freedom of having my own place and I suppose college was slightly more like Summerhill. You knew your teacher's first name. The students seemed really nice. I enjoyed living in London. I liked the markets, particularly in the Portobello area, but I'm not sure if London is a particularly good place to study. When you're a young person you just want to see the bright lights. I made friends: one in particular, a West Indian girl, and we've been good friends for a very long time. I enjoyed the fact that London was more cosmopolitan, the possibility of meeting people from all different parts of the world. Leiston's a very small little venture.

After 'A' levels I started a part-time diploma course in art in a college in Whitechapel, and that suited me because I could fit it around doing part-time jobs. It was a general foundation course – sculpture, pottery, photography; it was really good. I liked ceramics and decided that was what I wanted to specialise in. I applied for a degree course in ceramics in St. Martin's. I got a BA and then I tried to do my own work, but it wasn't enough to live off. I got a full-time job in a gallery, part of Liberty's, selling contemporary ceramics. I worked full-time to begin with, then part-time. I haven't gone on with my own ceramics. Since college I've just been working. Other people I know have had their own studios for a while, but it hasn't worked. I'm hoping that in the future I'll get more time to do it. I have been tempted to go into design, but not as a freelance; with a company. In future I would like to live and work abroad, in Africa. I would like to go to Sierra Leone where my father comes from. I haven't seen him since I was fifteen.

I later got a selling job in a store which is quite famous in the design world. It was quite aggressive and pressurised – you were given targets and you had to go out there and sell – but I quite liked it and I became reasonably successful at selling. Then I decided I wanted to make more use of my Art & Design degrees and enrolled on a postgraduate teacher training course. While on the course I did a teaching placement at a school in the East End, in Bow. I loved the students and the atmosphere of the area, which is so rich in history. After completing the PGCE [Postgraduate Certificate in Education], I decided to work in the East End and got a job at a school in Stepney, teaching Bengali boys. The entire school population was Bangladeshi. The students loved art and every year we achieved outstanding results in the art department. I found the work challenging, but fulfilling and worthwhile. I am currently in charge of an art department in a North London boys' school.

I don't think a feeling of social responsibility is something that comes from Summerhill particularly. I think you get that probably before you go; from your parents, I would have thought. Feeling that you want to contribute to society rather than take from it. It does come out at Summerhill as well. There is a strong community feel. Hopefully you should be helping everybody there to have a happy life – other people's problems are your problems. But it's also my mother's influence. It's not easy to see where you're getting different influences from. I'm still very close to my mother and spend school holidays with her in Yorkshire where she now lives.

I think Summerhill could make it difficult for some people to integrate into general society. A lot of work environments can be hierarchical and petty, and I would assume that some Summerhillians probably find that quite difficult. You do have to expect at work that somebody has authority over you, or you have authority, but I think that some Summerhillians don't ever get used to hierarchical systems in the work place because they've been brought up on the same level as everybody else. It's all very well to be independent, but you do need to be able to play at the game if you're in a company or a particular set-up. I can't speak for everybody, but I'm not sure if all Summerhillians feel that they want to "play" the game. Because they're used to being their own person.

I'm not sure if I've learnt to play the game. It can go against the grain. You see people being very hypocritical in hierarchical situations. There's a lot of deception and insincerity. That's one thing that a normal state school or public school will definitely prepare you for. I don't mean necessarily being a hypocrite but fitting into certain business systems. I don't think Summerhill does that so well. In some areas of creativity they want individuals, but in a lot of areas they're not wanting people who are going to be too much their own person. They need people who are very much just going to fit into certain spaces. It doesn't sound very nice, does it? In a way some Summerhillians can seem – I think it's a naiveté, which can be a drawback in certain situations. I think that's what I'm trying to say.

Summerhill offers a unique lifestyle. But I think there are other schools which can offer equally good opportunities, and maybe bring out more in people. It's a very small place. If I had children, I'd rather they were going to a bigger school with more facilities, somewhere like Dartington used to be. There were areas lacking at Summerhill. There could have been a much bigger music department. The drama was quite strong, but maybe it could have been even better. It could have had a dance teacher as well – ballet, sports, all those areas. It's disadvantaged by its size. When I left, it felt like a little capsule. You weren't having enough contact with the local community, for instance. No contact. I know that's the same for some public schools, but I still think there should have been more of a relation between the pupils in the school and their surroundings. What was going on in Leiston? There's Aldeburgh Music Festival – I don't remember us ever being taken there. We were taken to the Suffolk Show, but I felt there should have been more contact with the community, and more contact with people visiting – visiting tutors or new people coming in. Because in a way it becomes sterile. There just wasn't enough contact with the outside world. It was so institutionalised.

I wouldn't want a child of mine to be in a set-up like that as a teenager, because I don't think it's fair. It doesn't prepare you for the competition when you leave. The academic competition's really tough. It was reasonably tough when I left. Now it must be harder. I'm very glad that I went to Summerhill, and I'm glad I left when I did. Maybe it would have been better if I'd left a year earlier. It would have been easier settling in somewhere new. There does seem to be a strong tie with people from Summerhill; even though the person may not have been a particularly close friend, because it was such a small school you got to know them quite well. I see three or four Summerhillians, but I have other friends as well and I find them just as sincere.

There are a lot of good things in Summerhill that could be applied to other schools. Definitely. I think calling teachers by their first names is important and having more choice over subjects you can study (that's probably the case in most schools now) and giving children their own choice over rules. I think the attitude towards boyfriends is healthy. You're in close proximity. It should mean as teenagers you see boys as individuals rather than just boys. And I'd hope for the boys it would help them to see girls as individuals. I think Summerhill men are probably veering towards what's called the New Man. Probably nearer that than traditional. Whereas outside there is very much a ritual. I think that in secondary school it's very ritualised. A very sort of set pattern. I would hope that Summerhill men would not be so set in role models, so hypocritical; that they would have respect for their partners as whole human beings rather than as anyone they'd just managed to catch, as it were. I had a boyfriend at Summerhill and I have had a relationship with a Summerhillian since I left school, but I don't think that would be a consideration if I were to get married, because either you're suited to an individual or you're not.

I don't remember there being a big problem with smoking or alcohol at Summerhill. I don't know of any Summerhillians into drugs. I think that's a lot to do with peer group pressure. Similarly with heavy drinking. But even at college I was never exposed to drugs. My immediate friends didn't seem to be doing that. I drink socially. I think drinking wine is a very social thing, but drinking can become anti-social, especially with groups of men. Perhaps it's to do with male bonding. I don't know. But I think most Summerhillians don't have that sort of rugby characteristic. Maybe one or two have had a drink problem. I think that some men are driven to drink because they find it difficult to talk to people – friends, family.

It was interesting being brought up with children from different countries. Maybe that did help make me a broader person – being able to see past national stereotypes – but going to London contributed to that as well. I think it was an enriching experience having five friends who were all from different countries.

I probably have encountered racial prejudice since leaving Summerhill. Some people make cultural assumptions. That can happen in Summerhill too. Yes, generally speaking people can think they know something about another individual when they don't at all. Hopefully, coming from Summerhill, if it was working how Neill said it should, you wouldn't assume anything about anybody. You'd get to know them first.

What I feel I have gained from Summerhill (you can never really be sure if it's you or it's something that's come from Summerhill) is a feeling that you are not particularly bothered about whether you're pleasing people. It's a matter of whether you're satisfied with the job you've done. You feel that it's good enough. You have a good opinion of it yourself – and that is what matters in the end.

Postscript (2011)

I still work as head of art at an inner-city comprehensive school in London. I've spent the last five years combining work with caring for my mother, with whom I remained very close, travelling to Yorkshire every week to be with her. She died in May 2010.

Rhoda Goodall
1972-83

*It is a commonly-held view at Summerhill that children from secure,
happy homes have found the transition from home to boarding school
easier than others. This is borne out in the case of Rhoda Goodall who,
having spent her early years never out of the company of her parents,
while they travelled over Europe, arrived at Summerhill at a tender
age unable to speak more than two or three words of English, yet almost
immediately felt completely at home.*

Rhoda Goodall's parents, who are German, were travelling in England
when she was born, but a few months later they moved back to
West Berlin. Her father, who had been an architect, began designing
inflatables for festivals and Rhoda spent her early life on the road,
driving around Europe in a VW bus which she and her parents slept
in. "We travelled a lot and did everything together. When they went
out in the evenings I'd go with them." This nomadic life continued
until Rhoda was five and a half. "I suppose the German edition of
Summerhill had recently come out and they read it and liked the
sound of it – they didn't really agree with the German school system.
Also, I think because I was an only child they wanted me to grow up
in a family environment."

Rhoda visited the school with her mother and started in September 1972. Her mother stayed at a B&B in Leiston for the first week
and called in every day just to see that she was all right. "Apparently I
was straight in. Ena said to my mother, 'She's fine. She's a tough girl,
she'll manage.'" Although it was a big move for Rhoda, she made the
point that she had always felt secure with her parents and this made
the transition easier. "I've always been very close to my family and,
actually, the older I'm getting the closer we're getting. I always felt
loved. I never felt they were getting rid of me because they wanted to
get on with their own lives. It was nothing like that."

When she was seven Rhoda's parents split up. "It was only in
the holidays that I realised something was amiss. I actually looked

forward more to going back to school. I think probably the first few years after my parents separated I was upset, but going back to school made me feel loved anyway. One thing about Summerhill is it's like a family, a family that I never had in the sense that I don't come from a big family."

Rhoda remembers Neill, who died during her first summer holiday. "It was in the papers and my parents read it out to me. I was quite upset. He was such a lovely man and I'm really glad I did meet him. He was like a grandfather to everyone. He took the time to come round and speak to me in German and that made me feel more at home to start with. He was attached to everyone and he wanted to make sure – especially with people who were new – that they were doing all right. I remember him with his pipe, sitting in his armchair. That's the image I've got of him. He was a real character." Neill remained physically and mentally active to the end. "He used to play with us – ball or something – not running around, because he was nearly 90. But he was totally there, clear as a bell. If you said anything out of line he'd tell you to be quiet, or if you didn't want to do something, you had to give him a reason. In general he let you do what you wanted, up to a point, but he let you know when there was a right time and when there was a wrong time." Like other Summerhillians Rhoda emphasised that many outsiders misunderstand the nature of that freedom, confusing it with anarchy or, to use Neill's term, licence. "A lot of people think that Summerhill is not disciplined, but it is. It's up to you to get it together really; that's what a lot of people don't realise. If someone said something in a class and a teacher was in the middle of explaining something, you'd get told off, because otherwise you wouldn't learn. There were a few naughty children that came from pretty messed-up families and they were sent to Summerhill to sort of buck up really. And most of them did."

Rhoda recalled one of her housemothers, Sheila Philby, who had five children of her own. "I remember her in particular, because one Saturday in the San a whole load of us bought some food and after lights out we decided to have a picnic. We ate so much that we all felt pretty ill, and we made a lot of noise, and Sheila made us sit outside on the cold stairs in our pyjamas for about half an hour. Our backsides were freezing. It must have been winter. So that taught us a lesson and we didn't do it again, and that's why I can always remember her."

Rhoda remembers lessons as being well organised. To illustrate once again Summerhill's indifference to prevailing fashion in education, she recalls learning to read from the *Peter and Jane* books, by then regarded as beyond the pc pale in their supposed embodiment of white middle-class sexist values. However, from Rhoda's point of view "they were fine and I caught on quite quickly."

Afternoons were devoted to unsupervised play. In Rhoda's opinion the problem with a lot of adults she meets is that they haven't been able to play enough when they were children. "That's why there are a lot of frustrated people walking around. I look at children round here, where I live, and they can only play ball up and down the road. There are no playgrounds. At Summerhill we had a sand pit and swings, a big slide and a see-saw. There are a lot of fields and you can run around in the woods. We built dens." There was the famous 'Danë's Tree Hut', named after Danë Goodsman who had built it with a few of her friends – "It was quite difficult to get to, but we eventually sussed it out." The rope swing from the Big Beech has served as a rite of passage for many generations of Summerhillians. "I was about seven or eight when I first swung off. It was an absolutely huge piece of rope that was quite difficult to get to and it really pulls you off. Everybody would be encouraging you and you felt good when you did it."

Small children tended to play the same games, regardless of gender. "I used to play with cars when I was little, and not only with dolls, whereas round here where I live all the girls have got dolls and all the boys cars." However, although the girls did play football, only the boys continued it into their later years. "But I think it was a question of being more selective about what you liked rather than it being classed as a male sport."

One thing the children always dreaded was the visit of the school inspectors. "They used to make us feel like monkeys or look at us like creatures from another planet. So we used to really play up, to make sure that in their report they'd say, 'Oh, these are strange children.' As a child, if you have strangers coming round and looking at you, and they don't tell you why they are there, you worry. They'd be in the Meeting and there at lunchtimes and looking at your bedroom. Ugh. It wasn't very nice at all. You had no privacy. You felt like saying, 'This is our school, get out.'"

Like many Summerhillians Rhoda was a great reader. As small children they would be read to by their housemothers. "*Charlie and the Chocolate Factory* was one of our favourites, and *Puff the Magic Dragon*." She then went on to read for herself. "Fantasy stories at first. Not Mills and Boon things; never. When I became interested in going to English classes, I got into reading Charles Dickens and Emily Brontë. I liked Shakespeare when I was still young. I read modern authors as well – *The Catcher in the Rye, The Great Gatsby.* I've kept all my books – children's books, school books, homework books; some from when I was just learning to write, so you can hardly read the writing. They're something I wouldn't ever part with. I've always collected books and sometimes I'll read a book three, four times. All different things like *Lady Chatterley's Lover* or *Oliver Twist* – that's one of my favourites – or *Winnie the Pooh*, I loved that; *Jungle Book* – a real variety."

The library seems to have improved since Lucien Crofts's time. Rhoda remembers it as being well stocked. Television was no contender. "We were allowed to watch various programmes in the staff room: *Top of the Pops, Jackanory, Blue Peter, John Craven's News Round*, the occasional nature programme, and that was about it. TV was not important to us, not at all."

Latin was finally dropped from the curriculum during Rhoda's time. "Just when I wanted to do it. I don't know why they dropped it." In the time-honoured tradition of Summerhillians, Rhoda went through a phase of not going to lessons at all, though in her case it was fairly short-lived. "From about 14 to 15 I didn't want to do anything. Even my mother said I was terrible at that age." After her 'gap' year Rhoda began studying again and took some 'O' levels. "I did all right but I don't think it would have mattered where I'd gone; I wouldn't have been the sort of person who got 'A's."

Sports, horse-riding, Sunday rambles, drama, arts – all these things were enjoyable and fulfilling activities. Like Clare Harvie and Lucien Crofts, Rhoda has fond memories of Peter Wood, both as a potter and a loveable human being. He died during her time there. But her strongest feelings were for Ena. "I loved Ena very much and that's the main reason I visited Summerhill after I left – to see Ena. As children we thought she would always be there. She could be tough, but I think she had to be. It couldn't have been easy after Neill passed away. She ran the whole place herself." Like Lucien Crofts, Rhoda feels that Summerhill underwent a subtle change under Ena's governance. "I can't really pinpoint what changed, but it was different. Not worse at all, just different."

Children from outside seemed very against Summerhill. "Jealous, I think. I don't know what it's like now, but then it was 'Oh, you're from Summerhill, you must be really rich.' Because it's a private school everyone thinks you're loaded. I get these reactions sometimes now. It's awful. We did have a bit of trouble with the 'townies', as we called them. Not fights, but we were called snobs. I sometimes get called a snob nowadays. I always say what I think, that's what Summerhill definitely does for you. You don't beat around the bush and I think probably it can get you into trouble sometimes. It shocks quite a lot of people."

As the children got older they took on more responsibility for their lives. "It teaches you to be independent. From the age of 12 we were responsible for cleaning our rooms, doing the washing, stuff like that. I'm quite practical; I can sew, knit, crochet. I'm quite domesticated – I don't mind cleaning, ironing. I can fix a plug, put up shelves. But that also comes from my father; he always pushed me into becoming independent. If his car broke down he'd show me what was the matter. I'm not terrified of anything. I like challenges – keeps you on the ball. My ambition one day is to parachute out of an aeroplane. And I will."

Becoming a school officer or committee member increased people's sense of responsibility towards the community. "Neill always wanted the children to run the school. I took on the role of being an ombudsman a couple of times, and running the End of Term committee."

Like everything else in life, sex was talked about quite freely. "I think the attitude towards sex at Summerhill was healthy. Nobody got pregnant, yet girls down the road got pregnant all the time." Puberty was a difficult time for everyone. "Suddenly you're a man or a woman; it's quite freaky at the time but you soon get over that and just get on with it. Being with people you've known since childhood helps you through that stage."

Rhoda spoke of the infamous Channel Four *Cutting Edge* documentary. "I watched it with some people who went to Clifton College, which is totally the opposite of Summerhill. They nearly had heart attacks. They said, 'You really went to that school?' It was so difficult to say, 'This is not the school I went to. It's totally different.' It took me ages to convince them. My father sent me an article from *Der Spiegel* saying that the school might close. I had to sit down and really gulp for breath."

Some years ago Rhoda saw an advertisement in the paper asking for housemothers at Summerhill. "I nearly went for it, but in the end I thought, 'No, it won't be the same. It was my childhood.' When you talk about school, people ask you what it was like and I say, 'Well, it was great.' Most people I know didn't think their schools were great. Some say, 'I had a horrible life.' Well, I had a very happy childhood and it could have been totally the opposite."

After Summerhill

I left school in July 1983, had a couple of weeks in Germany with my mum and dad, and by August I was working. I didn't find it hard adjusting to the world outside. The best thing that happened was that I went straight into a job. I didn't have time to think, Oh, no, I've left school, what am I going to do now? I'll really miss it and I'm not going to get on with my life. I didn't have that at all. I knew I wanted to work with children when I left, so I organised an *au pair* job through friends in Switzerland. I spoke to the people on the phone, went there and ended up staying a year. It was excellent, a really good job. With the money I saved I went to Lanzarote in Spain for about nine months. My dad had bought a house there but he only came over once in that time. I lived in his house and learnt a bit of Spanish, learnt how to drive (on the wrong side of the road), worked in a restaurant, did a bit of nannying – all sorts, just to do different things. And a lot of bumming around meeting a lot of people.

I knew that other people were slightly different, so it wasn't a culture shock. I'd seen how people were in the holidays. I wasn't shocked, but was just surprised at how withdrawn a lot of people are. In every sense. Like nudity, for example, and the attitude of a lot of women to sex. They're quite sort of 'don't want to talk about it'. But with the majority of my friends I can have conversations about anything, whether they're male or female. Certain people you know you can't discuss certain subjects with, so you don't. Tried it once and it didn't work. I found older girls better to relate to than my own age, and I still find that sometimes now. Some people just seize up – about everything, everyday life.

While I was in Spain I applied to various nursery nurse colleges and one in Bristol accepted me. I started the course in September '85 and did that for two years. After that I worked for a couple of families in Bristol, on and off, for about three years. Then I decided I wanted to do something else. I hadn't had enough of kids as such, I just wanted to know what else I could do.

I find attitudes to children strange – definitely different from my own experience. When I occasionally mention that my parents used to take me everywhere when I was little, the reaction is, 'Oh, my goodness, didn't they get a baby-sitter?' No, my parents didn't believe in baby-sitters. And they just can't comprehend it. People have children; they go back to work a few weeks later. What's the point of having a child? Stay with it; at least until it goes to school. That's my view, and I'll stick to that. But I always listen to other people's view and if that's what they think that's fine. I'm not out to change their attitude.

I worked for a year in a clothes shop (where I found out that the customer is almost always wrong). In 1990 my then boyfriend got a job in Plymouth, so I moved down there. I got a job in customer service. I was dealing with German customers; on the phone all the time and going out for meals with them when they came over to the plant. When my boyfriend and I split up I came back to Bristol and did agency work. I started working for Avon Ambulance who offered me a permanent job in the accounts department, and I'm still there.

When I was at Summerhill I didn't really know what to think of marriage, because I'd seen so many people break up (a lot of the kids came from broken families) and because of my mum and dad. But I changed my mind straight away when I met Graeme. So many people I went to school with couldn't believe it. They're really surprised. I only know a couple of people from my time who've got married – it's quite rare – but quite a few have had children.

I can't really say what my children's education is going to be like till it happens. It's too early for that. I'd have to do a lot of research on whatever school I'd send them to. Although my school years were brilliant, I had a very good time, I sometimes wish I had taken more exams when I was there. But it's done now, and I don't feel any worse. Exams aren't the most important thing; people take you in interviews for what you know and who you are, not what's on paper in a lot of cases.

I don't think there's a perfect age to go to boarding school. For me, I don't think it was too young. I'd feel a bit of a failure if I had insecure children; I would think I hadn't done my job properly as a mother. The way a child turns out is usually the parents' fault, I think, but it probably depends a lot on their own childhood. Home background is very important. If you've got a bad atmosphere at home, it'll bring it out in the child when it's at school or with its friends, or whatever. A child should have a lot of play time – I'd definitely put that down as one of the priorities.

I don't think I would send my children to Summerhill. I'd like to see them grow up, till they go to college, then they can go wherever they want – to the North Pole. I think my mum sometimes feels guilty because she didn't see me grow up. I might change my mind. I don't know. Nobody really knows – whether they've gone to Summerhill or not – what sort of environment they'll want their children to grow up in. If you were to ask me in maybe six years' time I'd be able to tell you. But all the people I know from Summerhill, except perhaps one who was expelled, are all very stable. They've got good lives, jobs, stable family life. They're happy and satisfied.

Postscript (2004)

We now have two boys, aged four and eight, who attend the local village school and are both doing well there. Our elder son is given homework every week, but the school set the work in such a way that it is enjoyable and fun, rather than a chore, and we help him with it. In fact I think homework is a good thing as it shows us how he is getting on and what he is learning. Our younger son has just started school and is already taking in so many new things. The children are allowed to play a lot and he is happy. I still believe that play is an extremely important part of childhood. If my children were unhappy in any way, then I would do something about it, but I have no concerns at present.

Before I became pregnant with my second child I was studying to become an accountant, but have since decided that this is not the path I want to take in life. I have decided to become a translator – this will enable me to work at home, earn a living, and be around for the children. The best of both worlds, and I can finally escape the rat race of working in the city.

(2011)

I finally left my job as a financial controller with Avon Ambulance

Service about four years ago, and trained as a fitness instructor. I currently work in health clubs as a personal trainer.

Warabe Tatekoji
1981~90

The tendency towards specialisation and pigeonholing in education often makes it difficult for people with wide-ranging talents to fulfil themselves. Nationality or ethnicity can throw up further obstacles. Warabe Tatekoji, who was to do a degree in science and at the same time forge a career as a blues guitarist, was one of the first of a sizeable influx of students of Far East origin to enter an 'alien' environment. He is an example of how Summerhill helps some people to avoid what is for many a sense of restriction and awkwardness in the effort to find their path in life.

By the middle of the 1990s, Japanese, Koreans and Taiwanese made up one third of the Summerhill population, but Warabe was one of the first – and youngest. Warabe was born in 1973 in Hokkaido, a Japanese island north of the main island. His father was a lorry driver, then a taxi driver. When Warabe was five the family moved to Tokyo where Warabe's father began working in an institution for handicapped children. "He'd been doing that sort of work before becoming a lorry driver. In fact that's how he met my mother."

Warabe is an only child. When he was seven he started primary school. "It wasn't particularly nice. There was a certain amount of pressure and, according to my mother, when I came home and had to do some homework, I used to do it with tears streaming down my face."

Warabe describes his parents as very open-minded, "not just by Japanese standards, by any standards." His mother had discovered Summerhill shortly after leaving high school. "She found a book by Neill in a second-hand shop, picked it up and apparently the shop owner recommended it so she bought it, went home, read it, and thought, 'Wow, this is really good.' After that she got all Neill's books and thought, 'Well, this would be a great place if I ever had a child.'" Later she introduced the idea to Warabe's father. "Because he was a very liberal kind of person himself he thought, 'OK, if the child wants to go, then sure.'"

Before Warabe started school in Japan his parents told him he could either attend there or go to school in England. "I thought, 'No, I ain't going to England, it's too bloody cold.' Then, after I'd experienced what a Japanese school was like, I said, 'Remember that place you told me about. I want to go.'"

Warabe's parents put him on a plane with two older Japanese girls who were already going to Summerhill, a daunting experience for an eight-year-old. "They were about 10 and 12. I felt nervous, yeah. As soon as I was away from my parents I was in tears. But it was too late then, the doors were closed ready for take off. I was a very shy kid, so I didn't talk to these girls much. I was just looking out of the window – Ooh!"

Warabe's parents had given him some basic information about the school. "But the way I see it, the way my parents brought me up was very similar to the Summerhill way, anyway. So I was sort of prepared from the day I was born. They had to make a lot of personal financial sacrifice to send me to England. I think they had to borrow money here and there and are probably still paying off bits. They haven't told me anything about it, but they probably are."

It took Warabe some time to feel at home in Summerhill. "I seem to remember for quite a while waking up at two in the morning and feeling, 'Oh, oh, mummy, daddy – Ooh!' I suppose I wondered whether I'd done the right thing. But I was there, I wasn't going to fly back and it was all right after a time. There were rough patches, but it's always like that."

Warabe remembers picking up English fairly quickly – after about a term. "The Japanese girls started neglecting me after about two weeks, so I was forced to learn it, but at that age it's no problem; it just came through interacting. And there were other European kids there whose first language wasn't English – I seem to remember a lot of German people. I didn't have any culture shock. The biggest shock was being away from home. Otherwise, here it is and that's the way it is, and I've never been fussy about food."

After Warabe had been there a year, a few more Japanese started coming over. "They were a bit older than me and I started mixing with them. It wasn't too good. We started shoplifting and once we got caught." Ena was extremely stern with them. "Just her presence – Oh, I'll never do it again." During the holidays I was telling my parents about them and they said, 'Well, look, if you're going to go all the way to England and hang round with Japanese kids you might as well stay over here.' I took that quite seriously and after that I set myself apart slightly. I think the Japanese tend to have this communal thing; every nationality has it but Japanese maybe even stronger. They like to get together in a gang. I don't remember deliberately wanting to; it just happened."

Warabe's parents have always been a strong influence. "They always will be, I think. They've earned my respect in all that they've given me. The least I can do is respect them. I think one of the things I'd hate to do is to hurt them. I always try to digest what they say. At the time I might think, 'No, they're absolutely wrong,' but later on I think about it and see their point."

Homesickness alternating with schoolsickness persisted for several years. "The general trend was, I'd go to Summerhill, I'd feel homesick. Spend half a term there and not want to go home again. Then I'd go home and find myself wanting to go back to school. By the time the holidays were over I'd want to stay at home. That was the cycle. I think that went on, embarrassingly, till I was about 12. Until then I always found it very difficult to leave my parents, but once I'd got back to school it would be like, Yeah, whooo!"

Warabe's parents didn't ask him a lot of questions about Summerhill. "I think they saw that I was doing well and they had one-hundred-per-cent trust in the school. Didn't worry at all really, apart from the Japanese thing. I went to lessons for about a term, I think, because it was part of the daily thing. Get up in the morning, go to breakfast, play a bit and go to Class One. Most kids do at that age. We'd make things, play with Plasticine, paint, draw. I never had any formal lessons. After a term I started moving away from it, finding more interesting things to do, like mess about in the woods, climb trees, play games. Then I discovered woodwork, which was even better." The craft shop was open all the time and pupils could go in there and make whatever they wanted – including swords and guns for their war games. "There was a guy called Hopper on duty there. He'd just potter around, help you if you wanted it. If there was something you didn't know how to do, or there was a dangerous bit, he'd show you. He didn't give any formal instruction."

Initially, Warabe attended General Meetings without understanding anything at all, though the presence of Ena made an impact. "She struck me as a very powerful, strong woman. That's probably a lot of the kids' image of Ena. She'd always be there at the meeting and every now and then she'd say a few words. 'Ena's just spoken. Wow, yeah, yeah.' So she made a big impression. She wouldn't lay down the law, because Summerhill's a place where everyone has their say, but I think what she said, certainly you'd take up. She did have an influence. It wasn't her saying, 'It's got to be like this,' but it's a bit like how I would take notice of what my parents said."

Warabe started getting interested in lessons again when he was nearly 13. Initially his motivation was purely practical. "In the early days the lunch menu would be written on a blackboard outside the hatch. I used to go up to the hatch and stick my head through and say, 'Can I have everything, please?' And they'd give me everything on the menu. But there came a point when I thought, 'I don't particularly want everything.' I looked at the board and thought, 'What actually is for dinner today?' And I couldn't read the damn thing. Good grief, I can't read anything! So I thought I'd better learn. I went up to Boom, who was the English teacher at the time, and told him I wanted to start learning English. We spent quite a bit of time reading these silly little books about pirates. Embarrassing really. I'd never even read much Japanese before, except comic books." But he persisted. "I just really wanted to learn to read. I hadn't thought beyond that. These were tough times, but overall it was fine. I wouldn't consider myself a fast learner by any means. It's a bit embarrassing, I have to admit this, but I still find reading and writing a bit tricky and I've never got into reading much except text books. I was okay at that. The more I read, the more I became familiar with words and how things were spelt. And obviously I learnt enough to be able to pass exams." These days Warabe confines his reading to music magazines. "I'm not really fussed about it. I used to be, but nowadays I think, 'Nah, there are other qualities I have.'"

Warabe thinks the quality of the teaching at Summerhill was mostly satisfactory. "A lot of people, I seem to remember, would slag off various teachers, but I'm the kind of person who likes to take people as they are. Okay, they might not have been fabulous teachers, but I always feel they gave me something and I was quite happy myself. Maths I quite enjoyed, hence I went on to take astronomy at university." Physics in particular appealed to him. "Ever since I was a child I was the kind who liked to fiddle around with things, to find out how they work. With physics there is that manual side to it, making bikes and so on. It's all there."

His interest in chemistry waned after a couple of terms. "There was a whole bunch of kids who just wanted to make things explode and I got sick of it." The structured art lessons that he began going to when he was about 15 were more satisfying. "I think for some people at Summerhill that was quite strange, that formal approach, but I was quite happy and I scraped an A. I'd always had an interest in drawing – cartoons and stuff. When I was fairly young I made my own comics and found that immensely enjoyable. I remember winning a prize for a Halloween party competition for a comic strip which covered a whole wall. This was when I was about 9. At another Halloween party I made a wooden mask and dressed up as a robot and I won something for that as well. So I was quite chuffed.

"Part of what I liked about Summerhill is the fact that the big kids had this attitude towards the little kids, that if they were making things they would reward them. So that was great encouragement. I would say that the big kids had a more important influence than the adults."

Warabe remembers that there were always some children that you had to be wary of, and he did suffer a certain amount of bullying. "At the time it was pretty desperate, but now I look back and think, 'Ah, that's all part of it.' I don't regard it as something that's damaged me. I do remember one particular kid who, I think, was quite badly damaged by bullying, and after a time he left. But I like to think of these things in a positive way. Generally, if people were getting a really hard time, the community would step in. It would come up at meetings and tribunals and be discussed. And there were the ombudsmen. You could call them at any time."

After Summerhill

It wasn't a shock for me going to college. I heard from friends who were Summerhillians that they felt Summerhill didn't prepare them for the outside world. That's their view. But I felt I was prepared for it. I knew Summerhill was rather different, so in some ways I knew what to expect – there'd be more of a certain kind of discipline. But, then again, I was disciplined myself anyway because for the past two or three years I'd been studying. If I did notice any difference between me and the other students, I felt from time to time they were a little childish. Perhaps that's what happens if you've been suppressed and when you get to college there's a bit more freedom there. Probably it was easier for me to handle that freedom. I knew I wanted to work and get my exams.

I took maths and physics at Colchester and during my time there my personal tutor said to me, "You'd be the right type to go into research. You should go on to university." At that time I didn't even want to think about going to university. I just wanted to get everything over and done with and pursue my career in music – because at the time I had a few interests in certain blues bands around Colchester who were semi-professional. There was one band in particular, the band leader was saying, "We're about to become professional, would you be interested?" So I had my hopes up that I might suddenly be able to take up music as my career. Wow, great! So I didn't think about university, but then I talked to my parents about it and they said, "Why don't you?" They reckoned it would be good for me. We had a lengthy chat when they came over from Japan and I decided, yeah, I will – well, I'll try – and I did. I got in. And in the end the blues band just sort of died out.

I went to University College, London. I flipped through the prospectus and saw astronomy – "Oh, that's about the stars isn't it? That could be good." It was as easy as that. I had maths and physics at 'A' level. I thought it would be something interesting to do; find out what's going on up there. The first year was rather nice – because I was new in London, and I came here by myself; I made a whole load of new friends. I'd always wanted to take up martial arts, so I took up Kung Fu for a year and was really busy doing that. Then in the second year I thought, "This is all very fine but there's something missing here. What is it? It's the music. Where is it?" And then from that point I started concentrating more on music – and obviously studying – and the third year more music and more studying. I was quite willing to put time into studying because I knew my parents had put in a hell of a lot of money to keep me there – I couldn't get a grant because at that time I wasn't a resident. So there was no way I was going to let them down. I started something and I'm going to finish it, that's the attitude I had.

The final year was fairly intense. Then I got my degree, found a job, and carried on with music. But now I've settled down, I have a family and life very much revolves around them; though I am still playing music and always will. My ambition in music is still unchanged, to make a living. I'm not interested in becoming famous – I would like to be appreciated and I want to give people the joy and happiness that the music that I make and love brings to me. Music to me is such a strong force; it allows me to forget the problems that I'm having and reflect on good things.

Life has changed greatly for me since I've become a father; you start to see Summerhill from another angle, not just as a child going there, but also from a parent's point of view. Recently, more and more when I go back to Summerhill, I realise the happiness there is in children, and am constantly reminded of my own wonderful times there. For this reason I hope to be able to give my son the chance to go to Summerhill, much in the same way that my parents gave me the choice and the chance. It's some years yet before he'll be old enough to go to school, but these thoughts are always in the foreground of my mind. I am grateful that my wife also sees Summerhill as a healthy place for a child to grow up in and is with me on sending him there; since without both parents being happy with what Summerhill offers, the child could end up having a difficult time. I believe it is very important that both parents share a similar idea when it comes to parenting and education. I know that this is not always possible, but we parents must always try and do what's best for the child.

I still dream of Summerhill from time to time – not nearly as frequently as I used to, but it's still very much there as I live and breathe. Every day the experiences I had at Summerhill always make me feel good and confident inside. This is really important for me since I know some people who did not enjoy their schooling. In my view it seems a shame to spend one of the most precious times of your life (all times are precious, but childhood seems to be particularly unique) not enjoying it.

The main thing is that I'm happy about my life, and the way Summerhill has taught me, and I wouldn't change it in a million years.

Postscript (2011)

I am currently in the same job in IT that I started in 1999. For the past couple of years I have been studying to get certified. After work, I go to bed at the same time as the kids – I now have two sons, aged seven and four – and get up at 3am to study. Getting certified is an attempt to make sure that I am able to continue to support the family.

My wife and I were seriously going to try and send the boys to Summerhill this September, but we have decided to hold back a couple of years in order to allow us to save more money, and hopefully for me to get a better job with better pay as a result of my studies.

I have not been able to perform much live music in recent years, but continue to play at home, when possible. Since music is in my blood, I am not too worried about losing touch. It's more important now to concentrate on the family and working hard to try and fulfil my dream and ambition of sending my own kids to Summerhill. I have been in touch with the school over the years, and since my eldest son was born I have been back there almost every year in the hope of getting the boys feeling natural at Summerhill from the day that they start.

Abigail Taylor
1990 - 1995

It is often in the transition from primary to secondary schooling that many children come unstuck. From a small 'human-scale' environment they are thrust into a large factory-type organisation where they are conditioned to respond to Pavlovian bells and negotiate their way through a physical, intellectual and emotional labyrinth. It is at this point that many more sensitive children shut down. For Abigail Taylor the extended family environment of Summerhill was to prove a saving grace.

Abigail Taylor grew up in Cambridge where she attended a local primary school which she found perfectly all right. Her problems began when she went on to secondary school. "I found lessons difficult. You're only 12 when you first go and yet they're already going on about GCSE. It was awful."

As well as finding the workload burdensome, she developed a hatred of the teachers. "They acted very superior. Mum had heard of Summerhill and told me a bit about it and I thought it sounded like a nice alternative. When we visited I found it a bit strange, but also somewhere I could get used to. The first couple of weeks I hated it – 'Oh, my God, I've made the wrong choice!' Crying because I was homesick. After that I was fine. My housemother, who was from Greece, was very reassuring. I made friends and loved it there."

She found that most new kids got a hard time initially. "Petty things like getting your box broken into and sweets nicked. I shared a bedroom with four other girls, one English, two Japanese and one French. The French girl wasn't very nice to me. I think some people just test out new kids – think they're vulnerable and take advantage of that."

For the first month or so Abigail went to classes all the time, then stopped. "After I'd made friends it became boring going to lessons. It was more fun to run around playing all day." She didn't attend classes again for the next two and a half to three years, then began studying for GCSEs. "But I didn't really enjoy lessons, apart from drama. It wasn't anything to do with the teachers but, for example, maths – the course work drove me up the wall. I couldn't do it to save my life."

She got on well with most of the adults. "You know, you love some of them, don't particularly like others. I didn't see Zoë all that much, except in the meetings. Zoë can be quite fierce. We'd have arguments with her. She does go on a bit, but she's treated the same as everybody else and I think she has been fined sometimes for talking out of turn." Neill's widow, Ena, though semi-retired, was still a daunting presence at all the meetings and at supper. "She was very bossy. Everyone was scared of Ena. Well, not Zoë, but all the staff and kids."

Abigail went to most of the General Meetings, but it was about a year before she started speaking. "Before I left I'd spoken quite a lot, though I only chaired once – I plucked up the courage in my last term. I thought it was something I should do before I left. It went fine, but you get sick of standing up all the time and telling everyone to be quiet. Sometimes the chairs walked out in floods of tears because everyone was being really annoying; wouldn't shut up. You got some days like that, but most of the time it was okay. A few people chaired a lot. They liked it and they knew how to do it. It was pretty evenly divided between boys and girls."

The separate Tribunal, however, she found generally boring. "It was mostly little kids bringing each other up for poking and hitting. Petty little things. I think most of the older kids found it boring. Then for a while it became fun. It shouldn't have been, but it was at a time when people were running around outside all night and getting drunk in the town. Quite a few people got sent home for about a week, and if they carried on afterwards they got chucked out. Only Zoë can expel someone. It is quite disturbing when people get expelled, especially if it's your good friend. I never got sent home, but I was fined for harassing people, going down town when I wasn't supposed to; occasionally for drinking, but nothing very serious. A few little kids got into trouble with the police for shoplifting, but in the last couple of years of my time there nobody was doing anything very bad. I think it happens when there are a lot of new kids together and they break out."

The very worst time occurred after Abigail's first term when the Channel 4 film crew was present. "They were there for about six months and for half the time all the rules were dropped." [It has happened every so often throughout Summerhill's history that the General Meeting has voted to abolish all the rules – see interview with Ethan Ames]. "Everyone was running riot and there were a few Americans who found it difficult to get on and were causing trouble. There were two very strong-minded, powerful girls who fell out and formed rival gangs which fought one another. In the end Zoë chucked one of them out and quite a few people who were in the gangs left, so it settled down."

After the film crew left, rules were re-introduced and Summerhill began to pick up. "If you get a strong group of older kids it helps. I think we were quite strong before I left. Generally the laws work well and the community works as a whole – it's been going on for over 70 years, so probably that has a lot to do with the tradition that's been built up. One of the secretaries found lots of really old General Meeting minutes books and, apart from the money, you could see things really hadn't changed that much. Among the little kids definitely it hasn't changed. The system's changed a bit, obviously, since Neill died, but I think that children's nature hasn't changed, or the basic idea hasn't changed."

One thing that has changed quite a lot since Abigail left is the school's appearance. "When I first came it was really run down. House was just about falling apart. We had squeaky old bunk beds; now they've got pine bunk beds, a new office, new classrooms, and all the rooms have been done up. It's really posh. The kitchen's like a spaceship." Abigail is not so sure that this is an improvement. "I think it was better before, because you could mess it up and it didn't really matter too much. But now there are stricter rules about keeping your room tidy. Part of Summerhill was not having to keep your room clean and tidy. Now you're not allowed to write on the walls;

I know you shouldn't, but it's the kind of thing you do when you're younger – get it out of your system."

The long school holidays were a problem at first. "It was so boring at home. There was nothing to do because all my friends were in different parts of the world and I lost contact with people I had been friends with before. It was a bit of a shame really. Sometimes Summerhillians would come and stay with me or I'd stay with them or we'd go away together."

Boarding was definitely a plus. "Living with other people you get to know them really well. You did get depressed or angry sometimes – you go though all your hormonal changes, get pissed off, angry, upset. I think Summerhill is a good place to go through all that. Puberty – you're on your own with it really – but there's always people there to help you along. You do sometimes get in a situation where you hate people. Arguments, fights. When you're living in a room with someone you get annoyed with them being there all the time, although the lack of privacy didn't really get me down till I was older, and by the time I was 15 I had my own room, which was the time I really wanted it."

There was friction with the local kids. "There have been quite a few incidents where people from Summerhill have got beaten up. I think they're probably jealous of Summerhill, but they always go on about it, saying a load of awful stuff. It got particularly bad after the documentary. People were threatening Henry: 'We'll chop your head off.'" [This refers to the infamous scene where Henry Readhead was filmed decapitating rabbits. What wasn't explained was that the rabbits were dying of Myxomatosis – a particularly horrible death. Henry was putting them out of their misery]. "I think he coped all right. A bit upset. We used to go down town to the shops and they'd call us names – 'Summerhill bitches' and stuff like that. They'd know we were from Summerhill because we looked different from everyone else. Didn't care so much about clothes. The local girls were all wearing high heels and make-up, so it was quite easy to tell us apart. And there are lots of different nationalities among us."

Abigail was sympathetic to the plight of Leiston kids. "They get really bored, so they resort to drugs and harassing Summerhillians. They just live in their small town all their lives. There should be more clubs and activities for them. I think we had a broader life."

For a time a few pupils were smoking dope. "It got discovered and one of them got chucked out. He got a warning but carried on doing it. I've smoked dope but it's not something I do. I think alcohol might be even worse in some ways. I go to the pub after college sometimes and have a few drinks, but not all that much."

A recurring question is the extent to which children with learning difficulties or severe emotional problems can be integrated into Summerhill. It seems that some can and some can't. "There were a few disturbed kids when I went there – a bit strange; a bit backward. Most of them were all right, but I think some of them got a hard time. They shouldn't really get a hard time at Summerhill, but they do. I think it probably happens less in Summerhill than in other schools, but some people would pick on them or make fun of them. There were some very rebellious kids there as well. People who really broke out and did it for years, though I think by the time they were 16 they were all right. One of my friends was really awful for years and years, but he's fine now."

Summerhill's greatest deficiency, in Abigail's opinion, is its lack of sports facilities. "It was great for small kids, climbing trees and running around the woods, but they don't have enough sport for older kids. Even though I wasn't into sport, a lot of people were, so they should have had a proper sports teacher. I think that would go down well."

In her last year, Abigail attended, together with one of the Summerhill houseparents, an international conference of democratic schools held at Sands School in Devon. She was taken aback by the hostile reception and criticism of Summerhill. "They were awful. They were having a go at us for not being free enough. Both the kids and the teachers, but mostly the adults from Sands School. Nobody stuck up for us. I didn't know what to say. They were throwing all these questions at us like why do we have separate boys and girls rooms. Why? Why shouldn't we? I think, perhaps, because we were the creator of all free schools they felt competitive towards us. They wanted to be better. I don't think Summerhill gives a toss really." Abigail was not impressed. "The kids at Sands don't have to go to lessons, which is the same as Summerhill, but I didn't really see that many similarities. It's a day school, which is really different. You get more involved when you're boarding. The kids at Sands have even more power than we do. They're allowed to sack and hire teachers. I find that bizarre. I think Summerhill's got it right. If you've got too much power it can go wrong."

Abigail stressed the gender equality at Summerhill. "We didn't feel dominated by boys. I think it is different outside. There were a few girls who wore make-up at Summerhill, but a lot less than the girls in town. I was the only girl at college who didn't wear make-up. It's just that I don't know why they do – if it's to please the boys, or they do it to make themselves feel good. I don't wear make-up because I don't see the point. You don't get any pressure at Summerhill – if you want to wear fashionable clothes it's all right, and if you don't it's all right. It doesn't have any effect on the way people treat you."

It was not until her last year or two that Abigail discovered what she was interested in and wanted to do. "They weren't doing drama when I first came, but then it started. I was probably about 15. We had improvisation and acted in EOT [end-of-term] plays, and we went on trips to the National Theatre, the theatre in Ipswich, and Stratford. *The Little Shop of Horrors*, which I did in my last year, was about the only scripted play we did. We were practising all term, which got a bit annoying, but it worked well in the end." Leaving Summerhill with the knowledge that this was what she wanted to do, Abigail applied to study drama and was accepted for a two-year course by a Bristol college.

After Summerhill

I didn't have any idea of what college would be like. It was harder work than I first thought it would be, but I still enjoyed it. I didn't work very hard at Summerhill because I didn't really enjoy anything much except drama, but because it was just drama I was doing in college, it was fun, so I did more. I found I didn't mind writing essays and was okay at it. I couldn't believe how many GCSEs kids had to take in ordinary schools. I took five, whereas most of them had taken 10 or 12. Why? You don't need them.

It was a shock at first, settling into college. It was totally different from Summerhill and it took a while to get used to. People tended to be different and I found making friends quite hard. A lot of people on my course were in their twenties and I tended to like them better. The younger ones seemed a bit – well, young. They were still breaking out, I think, and at Summerhill we'd already done that. Although there was one girl about my age who became a good friend.

I think I've got more of an overview of Summerhill now, because I've had more life experience. I have come to appreciate it, but only recently. I had a great time there, but there were certain aspects I was slightly resentful about when I first left. Summerhill gives you a lot of education in personal growth, but at the same time it makes it difficult to fit into the outside world. I felt resentful that I was different – that I was this odd person – and at that age you just want to fit in. Making the transition from school to college is difficult anyway. I didn't live with Summerhillians any more, and when you're not surrounded by other Summerhillians you feel a bit isolated. I was in quite a rough area of Bristol and maybe that had something to do with the difficulty I had. Making friends, living with my mum in a completely new city – everything was different.

I didn't discuss Summerhill with other people. Not because I was ashamed of having been there, but I didn't want to appear different. I enjoyed the college course. I got my B-tec National Diploma in Drama and looking back I think it was a very good course. The guy who ran it was excellent and knew what he was doing.

After I'd finished college I was still keen on becoming an actress or doing something in theatre, so I did a few auditions for drama school but didn't get in. Then I applied to do a drama degree – half academic, half practical – and got in to Aberystwyth on a three-year

BA. I liked it, but a lot of it was very academic. I did okay, but I also saw a side of drama and acting that I didn't want to enter into – getting judged so much on your appearance; people stabbing one another in the back to get the part they wanted; sucking up to the director. It's very hard to make it as an actor and you have to be very pushy and competitive, which is not really in my nature.

I had worked a bit with kids in drama in college, in the Special Needs department, and at uni. I did a TIE [Theatre in Education] module which developed my interest further. Going into schools made me change my mind and direction. Drama is a great therapeutic tool. That aspect of creativity and expression is wonderful. So my ambition to be an actress fell away. For my dissertation I did TIE and from reading around I got interested in dramatherapy, though I didn't want to do it straight away. I saw it more as a long-term thing.

I found Aberystwyth a much easier place to be than Bristol. It's a small place – tiny. It felt safe. And that's when I really started to feel at ease with people. I had a whale of a time. It was great. I didn't think about Summerhill at that time – it wasn't in the forefront of my mind. I was interested in what I was doing – learning new things, experiencing new things, making new friends. It was an enjoyable student lifestyle. I suppose I did talk to a few friends about Summerhill and they said it sounded cool. I think drama students are in a class of their own, so I fitted into that. I met a lot of people from different backgrounds. They were all fairly crazy – more free and out there; independently-minded. I liked that.

Once I'd graduated I knew I didn't want to go straight on to do an MA as a lot of people were doing. I wanted to get some hands-on experience working with kids with special needs. There wasn't enough going on in Aberystwyth, so I moved to Brighton with my best friend from Summerhill. I got jobs working with kids with various types of special needs – mental and physical, disabled kids in wheelchairs – on an after-school basis, then fell into working with kids with EBD [emotional and behavioural difficulties]. I also worked for a bit in a Montessori school. It was more like a crèche. I did a few drama workshops and games, a lot of art projects, juggling.

I do find it easy to get on with little kids. I see them more as equals rather than people you need to teach or discipline. I can talk to them on that level. They know what's going on from a very young age – they've got a lot of understanding. But a lot of people patronise them. Summerhill kids are never spoken down to as if they were some subordinate form of life. Also, there were some people with special needs at Summerhill. So I think that's helped me working with kids now. I don't see EBD kids as aliens that I need to cure. They are still human beings that I can talk to and relate to. They're not just case studies. I relate to them more on a personal level. I do get a good reaction from them. I really do. I don't want to blow my own trumpet, but I always get along with them, more as a friend than a teacher or carer. There are, for example, some people coming into this area who work solely from textbooks – they don't have hands-on experience. And when they do confront the reality it's a total shock to them. A lot of people with years of experience are fantastic, but I've noticed it more with individual therapists. The kids are just case studies. They've no experience of their home life or what they are like every day. It's slightly dubious.

At present I'm working for an agency and before that I worked abroad for eight months, initially in Indonesia, then in Thailand. In Indonesia I taught English in various different schools and in Thailand I worked in an orphanage – a community – and taught English, art and drama. The project originated in India. The only thing I can compare it to is Hare Krishna, but it's not specifically religious. It's run by Dadas and Didis, the equivalent of monks and nuns, who wear orange. Dada is masculine, Didi feminine. They're doing self-realisation through social work. Their initial training is a lot of meditation and yoga and stuff like that. Then they're sent to different countries where they're given a bit of land and their brief is to set up an educational project or village.

My own Didi was an Italian who set up the community over 15 years ago. Then someone else established a school for the children. It's an amazing place; very beautiful. The education is quite free and relaxed and a lot of the aspects reminded me of Summerhill. It goes under the name Bandarah Neo-Humanist Foundation, but the overall title is Anandamaya. I didn't know much about the philosophy before arriving, but I embraced it once I got there. I took up meditation and yoga, gave up smoking and drinking, and as they are vegetarian I also gave up meat. I became initiated into it and was given a Sanskrit name.

It's the kind of place where no one tells you what to do. You just ask and eventually find your feet. You don't get paid, but in return for teaching in the school I was given accommodation and food. It was great; I really admired it. I'm not a great believer in self-sacrifice, but I was impressed. The people who run it seem very calm and at peace with themselves. Not enlightened exactly, but something very special. There were also a number of volunteers, like me, from various countries. I met some lovely people. I felt at home and it was almost like being at Summerhill. It's a community – relaxed, not like a missionary place. Kids can do what they want, although they are asked to meditate twice a day. But it was fine. They're all really amazing kids; really chilled out. They're meant to do the meditation as part of being there, so they just do it and I think it helps. They come from different parts of Thailand, many from near the Burmese border, and there are some Burmese refugees. Most are orphans but there are also some destitute mothers with babies. The mothers looked after the babies, and the older kids looked after the younger ones. They're really happy that they've got somewhere to live and they've got food and clothing. I'm sure there was emotional scarring but there isn't a lot of time for psychoanalysis. Some children were very ill and have died since I left – from HIV or the effects of malnutrition.

Going away was a revelation. It made me think about the way we live our lives and what we worry about in the West. I did get quite ill. I got a parasite which caused abscesses and left me quite run-down and anaemic. When I got back I had to go to hospital for treatment. I want to go back, but I've got debts here. Once I've saved some money I want to spend a few more years travelling, then come back and do an MA in dramatherapy. It's only been available as an MA over the last 10 years, I think, so I need to find out what opportunities there are for a qualified therapist. I'd be interested in going into different institutions – hospitals, children's homes, special needs schools.

I did consider working at Summerhill for a while, thinking about my career at the time, "I'm gaining experience but it's not really going anywhere." So I gave Zoë a ring. She said, "We'd really like to have you. We like to encourage ex-Summerhillians to come and work here because they know how the place works." There was a houseparent leaving so I was going to take over his job, which would have also given me an opportunity to run drama workshops or whatever the kids were interested in – if they were at all.

I was going to do it, when this guy decided not to leave. I was in two minds anyway, because it's quite a big commitment and you don't really have a life outside. It leaves you quite stuck. It may still happen, but I'm more interested in earning money to go travelling. I know people who went back to work at Summerhill for a bit. One went for two/three years. I think for him it probably wasn't such a good idea to stay so long. It was almost him not wanting to leave in the first place and then going back and carrying on from where he left off. Not having much life experience in between. It's still a possibility for me, but not now.

There are quite a few Summerhillians living in Brighton and I do mix socially with them sometimes. I shared a house with a few of them for a bit. It does ease social living; it was similar to being back in Summerhill. But I don't find it hard living with other people. I'm older and I can adjust. Recently I've begun to want my own place, but I can't afford it. The way things are it's impossible for anyone my age to buy a house in this country. I don't know whether I could earn a good living as a dramatherapist. I'm not going into it for the money. Maybe if I went to Hollywood and became a dramatherapist to the stars. I've no idea, but the American ideal doesn't appeal to me. I'm more interested in developing countries and in behaviour problems and childhood development.

There are obviously differences between kids here and in the developing world. They see education as a means of getting a job. At Summerhill it was about what's right and what's wrong: moral issues. My mother was paying for me to have the choice of maybe not even having an education. For me to try to explain that to kids who can't afford to go to school, let alone college and university, and have to get a job selling nuts or something – from that perspective they'd go "What?" But when you're living in England it's different. Everything about living in a developing country is different. When it is developed – if it ever is – then maybe it will change. At the moment they respect you because you're from a richer country. You must be intelligent and knowledgeable because you've got money and education. You get respect for that.

Most of the Western volunteers I've met in developing countries are decent people who want to experience a bit more from life and see what the whole world's about. They have compassion. I wouldn't call myself a do-gooder. It isn't my mission to save the world. I got a lot out of it for myself as well.

All in all I would say Summerhill has been an advantage to me in what I'm doing now. With drama I was allowed to explore my creative side all the time. We did a lot of plays. My friend and I used to go round the school dressed up as characters and take on different personas. That kind of thing you are allowed to do at Summerhill, which is bloody amazing. That is what Summerhill has done for me – developed my creative side. It's also made me interested in children and how they are brought up – in education and behaviour. Now I'm trying to combine it all – all that I'm interested in – combine drama and therapy and people.

One of my favourite stories when I was younger was by John Burningham. It was about a boy and his mum who plant a plum tree which grows into a giant plum tree. Then, later, when I was looking through my old childhood books, I discovered he'd gone to Summerhill. That gave me a strange feeling to realise one of my favourite children's authors had been to Summerhill.

I would love to have children myself one day, but I'm not quite ready for it yet. I don't think I would send them to Summerhill, because I think I've learnt enough from Summerhill and the world and my own experiences to give them the benefit of that in their own home. It was an advantage for me going away because I was having an awful time at school and I didn't have a big family. Summerhill provided that. But I think I could create that atmosphere in my own family, particularly if there were other Summerhillians and their kids living near. If they were having a hard time in school, and I had the money, then I'd consider it.

I think for me personally the most beneficial aspect of Summerhill would probably be the opportunity to work on myself. I was able to explore myself emotionally, and spiritually, rather than what I could do academically. Explore myself as a person. Understand myself as a person and how I related to others. That's what is really important in life and not many people get the opportunity to do that.

Postscript (2011)

I subsequently gained an MA in Dramatherapy at Roehampton University, on a three-year part-time course. I currently live in London where I have recently obtained work delivering dramatherapy to children with Autistic Spectrum Disorder and other learning and communication difficulties. I also run a dramatherapy group in a West London refugee community centre for adult refugees and asylum seekers. With a business partner, I hope to open a creative arts therapy centre in Kampala, Uganda. At the moment we are in the very early stages of setting up a voluntary trust which will eventually become a charity.

Brief Chronology
of A.S. Neill and Summerhill

1883   A.S. Neill born in Kingsmuir, Scotland.

1897   Leaves school and works as clerk and draper's assistant.

1898   Taken on by his father as pupil teacher in Kingsmuir Village School.

1903   Fails entry exam for teacher training college. Obtains work as "authorised" teacher.

1906   Passes first part of acting teacher's certificate. Becomes assistant master at a school in Fife.

1908   Passes second half of university entrance exam. Reads English at Edinburgh.

1912   Graduates with MA; pursues career in journalism.

1914   After outbreak of World War I is appointed head of Gretna Village School.

1915   Publishes *A Dominie's Log*, which becomes a best-seller.

1917   Called up for military service, commissioned, but not drafted abroad. Meets Homer Lane and visits The Little Commonwealth.

1918   Little Commonweath closed. Neill joins staff of King Alfred School in Hampstead, London.

1921   The International School opens in the Dalcroze Centre, Hellerau, near Dresden, with Neill as principal

1923   School moves to Sonntagsberg, Austria.

1924   School moves to a house on "Summer Hill" in Lyme Regis.

1927   School moves to Leiston, Suffolk, acquiring the name Summerhill. Neill marries Lilian Neustatter [Mrs Lins].

1940   School evacuated to Ffestiniog, Wales.

1944   Lilian Neustatter dies.

1945   School returns to Leiston. Neill marries Ena Wood.

1946   Zoë, only child, born.

1950   Neill refused entry to United States on grounds of communist sympathies.

1960   *Summerhill: A Radical Approach to Child-Rearing* published in USA.

1961   Influx of American pupils saves school from financial ruin.

1973   Neill dies. Ena continues to run the school.

1985   Ena retires and Zoë takes over as principal.

1999   After OFSTED inspection a Notice of Complaint is served. School lodges formal appeal.

2000   Complaint is withdrawn. Summerhill is, in Zoë's words, "safer than it has ever been".

2011   Summerhill celebrates "90 Years of Freedom".

Glossary of Summerhill Terms

Beddies Officers
Summerhill students who are elected to serve as officers ensuring that everyone observes the bedtime rules. There are different bedtimes for different age groups

The Big Beech
A large beech tree with a rope swing in the grounds of Summerhill that for successive generations has served as something of a rite of passage for pupils. There is a crutch for an easy swing and also a board for the more ambitious, higher up the tree.

Carriages
Originally two out-of-use railway carriages purchased by Neill for use as temporary sleeping accommodation for older pupils. Subsequently replaced by long huts, but still referred to as the "Carriages". Older children are called "Carriage kids".

EOT
End of term. Each term a themed party is organised by the EOT committee. In the house, the lounge is closed off for the last week of term and the room is decorated in secret.

FOST
The Friends of Summerhill Trust. A charity managed by Old Summerhillians, which produced a magazine. It started in the 1980s and survived for about a decade.

GM or General Meeting
Now more often referred to as simply "the Meeting". A weekly parliament, or moot, where the whole community gathers to discuss items of interest and make decisions on matters affecting the social life of the community.

Gram Committee
An elected committee for organising dances. Pupils were originally in charge of a wind-up gramophone and records. It retains its original name.

The Hockey Field
This field, adjacent to the main house, was originally used by the students for hockey practice and home matches with other schools. It has retained its name, although hockey has not been played there for many years.

House
The main building where students, mostly the younger children, have their bedrooms; usually no more than five to a room.

Houseparent
Houseparents are responsible for the practical and welfare issues to do with the children in their particular group. They are not teachers.

Kids
Children at Summerhill are traditionally referred to by each other and staff as big kids or little kids.

Laws
Rules at Summerhill are referred to as "laws".

Ombudsmen
Specially elected pupils or adults who are available to help resolve conflicts in the community. They often represent little kids in the meeting.

PLs or Private Lessons
These were in fact voluntary one-to-one therapeutic meetings with Neill in the manner of a talking therapy. Some Old Summerhillians say they benefited greatly from them, others not at all. Neill used the practice less in later years.

San
Originally built as a sanatorium for pupils who were sick, it was so seldom used that it was taken over as sleeping quarters.

Schulgemeinde
Precursor of the General Meeting, introduced at the International School where the principle of one person one vote was established and maintained. Retained its title at Lyme Regis but eventually changed to General Meeting.

Summerhill Joker
A magazine or broadsheet produced for a while in the 1930s and 40s.

Tribunal
At times in the school's history items concerned with anti-social behaviour have been referred to a weekly tribunal. Anyone can attend and vote on "fines" which may be financial but could also be tasks imposed, activities denied, or simply being banned from leaving the school grounds.

Appendix
People and places referred to in interviews

J.D. Bernal (1901-71)
Father of Mike Bernal. Nicknamed "Sage". Eminent crystallographer and left-wing thinker; author of several books including *The World, the Flesh and the Devil* and *The Social Function of Science.*

Michael Boulton
Former pupil. Subsequently a dancer with Sadler's Wells Theatre Ballet in 1940s. Appeared in performances with Margot Fonteyn, Moira Shearer, Beryl Grey.

John Burningham (b. 1936)
Former pupil. Successful children's author and illustrator, whose many books include *Trubloff: The Mouse Who Wanted to Play the Balalaika* and two books about *Mr Gumpy*, a character inspired by A.S. Neill.

Ivor Cutler (1923-2006)
Former teacher (1950s). Well-known poet, broadcaster, singer-songwriter, humorist. Recorded numerous sessions for John Peel's radio show and appeared in the Beatles' *Magical Mystery Tour.*

Émile Jaques-Dalcroze (1865-1950)
Founder of Eurythmics ([see below]. Established Dalcroze Centre in 1910 at Hellerau, near Dresden, where, in 1921, Neill began his International School.

Len Deighton (b. 1929)
[see Robert Muller interview]. Author of many thrillers, cookery books and histories of World War II. Three of his thrillers were turned into films starring Michael Caine, most notably *The Ipcress File.*

Eurythmics
System of teaching musical concepts through movement, devised by Dalcroze [see above].

Lucy Francis (d. 1969) Former houseparent and teacher. Joined Neill at Lyme Regis and left Summerhill in 1944 to found Kingsmuir School (named after Neill's birthplace) for very disturbed children. Kingsmuir closed in 1970.

John Graham-White (1913-2008)
Former teacher (1936-38). Eminent clinical psychologist. His experiences at Summerhill, where he acquired the nickname "Jasper", inspired him to train in psychoanalysis. In 1958 he became the first clinical psychologist in Northern Ireland.

'Grimey' – Leslie Grimes (1898-1983)
Cartoonist mentioned in R. Muller interview. In 1927 he became political cartoonist for the *Star* and in 1932 began his series *All My Own Work*.

Hellerau
Site of the International School, a garden city, in the district of Dresden, which was built early in the 20th Century.

John Holt (1923-85)
American teacher and writer on education and an admirer of A.S. Neill. His best-known books are *How Children Fail* and *How Children Learn*, which were at one time required reading in teacher training colleges.

'Jak' – Raymond Jackson (1927-97)
Cartoonist mentioned in R. Muller interview. Worked for *London Evening Standard* from 1952.

Mrs Lins – Lillian Neustatter (1871-1944)
First wife of Neill, who helped him establish the International School. Before Neill she was married to Otto Neustatter, a German physician and Chair of the Society for the Fight Against Quackery. Her sister, Ethel, was a well-known Australian novelist who wrote under the name of Henry Handel Richardson.

Ishbel McWhirter (b. 1927)
Former pupil. Successful artist. 'Discovered' at Summerhill exhibition held at the Arcade Gallery, London in 1945. Studied under Oskar Kokoschka. Commissioned portraits include

Germaine Greer, Melvyn Bragg, A.S. Neill

Krishna Menon (1896-1974)
[see Elizabeth Pascall interview]. Indian politician, journalist, friend of Nehru. Resident in England 1929-47. Co-founder, with Allen Lane, of Penguin Books. Indian Defence Minister, 1957-67.

Leslie Morton (1903-87)
Former teacher and notable left-wing historian. Books include the famous *A People's History of England,* 1938.

Rebecca de Mornay (b. 1959)
Former pupil. Hollywood actress. Starred in *The Hand that Rocks the Cradle.*

Edwin Muir (1887-1959)
Famous Orcadian poet. Accompanied his wife, Willa, to the International School, 1921. Translator, with Willa, of Kafka. His collected poems were published in 1991.

Willa Muir (1890-1970)
Former teacher at the International School, 1921. Writer and translator, wife of Edwin Muir. Books include two novels, *Imagined Corners* and *Mrs Ritchie.*

Ralph Muller (1933-2007)
Former pupil, brother of Robert Muller. Eminent parasitologist and former Director of The International Institute of Parasitology, St. Albans. Author of *Worms and Human Disease* and *Medical Parasitology.*

Ena Neill (1910-97)
Neill's second wife. After his death she continued as principal of Summerhill.

Ulla Otte
Former houseparent. Arrived at Summerhill when it was in Wales during the Second World War. Originally employed as a cook, she set up a handwork class which she ran for more than 20 years. One of the longest-serving staff members at Summerhill, and remembered with great affection.

Zoë Readhead (b.1946)
Daughter of A.S. Neill and Ena Neill. Current principal of Summerhill School.

Evelyn Williams (b. 1929)
Former pupil. Left Summerhill at 14 to study at St. Martin's School of Art. Successful painter and sculptor. Now in her 82nd year and still exhibiting.

Peter Wood
Son of Ena by her first husband and stepson of Neill. A skilled potter, he studied under Bernard Leach and later taught at Summerhill.

Suggested Further Reading

Books by Neill

A Dominie's Log, Herbert Jenkins, 1916

Summerhill, Gollancz, 1962

Talking of Summerhill, Gollancz, 1967

Neill! Neill! Orange Peel!: A Personal View of Ninety Years,
Weidenfeld & Nicolson, 1973

Letters by Neill

Beverley R. Placzek (ed.), *Record of a Friendship: Wilhelm Reich and
A.S. Neill*, Farrar, Strauss, Giroux, 1981

Jonathan Croall (ed.), *All the Best, Neill: Letters from Summerhill*,
Deutsch, 1983

Books about Neill and Summerhill

Jonathan Croall, *Neill of Summerhill: The Permanent Rebel*,
Routledge & Kegan Paul, 1983

Matthew Appleton, *A Free Range Childhood: Self Regulation at
Summerhill School*, Foundation for Educational Renewal, 2000

Mark Vaughan (ed.), *Summerhill and A. S. Neill*, Open University
Press, 2006